THE
ASIAN
AMERICAN
CENTURY

The Edwin O. Reischauer Lectures, 2000

THE
ASIAN
AMERICAN
CENTURY

WARREN I. COHEN

MULTICULTURAL
STUDENT PROGRAMS

HARVARD UNIVERSITY PRESS

Cambridge, Massachusetts
London, England • *2002*

Library of Congress Cataloging-in-Publication Data

Cohen, Warren I.
    The Asian American century / Warren I. Cohen.
      p. cm.
    "The Edwin O. Reischauer lectures, 2000."
    Includes bibliographical references and index.
    ISBN 0-674-00765-4 (alk. paper)
    1. United States—Civilization—East Asian influences. 2. East Asia—
Civilization—American influences. 3. East Asia—Foreign relations—
United States. 4. United States—Foreign relations—East Asia. 5. United
States—Foreign relations—20th century. I. Title.

E169.12 .C546 2002
303.48'27305—dc21   2001039635

FOR PAUL A. COHEN

Probably wiser, certainly older

ACKNOWLEDGMENTS

When I received the invitation to deliver the 2000 Reischauer Lectures at Harvard University, I was both delighted and troubled: delighted because it was a great honor, troubled because my audience would be familiar with the writing that had merited the invitation—and bored if I repeated it. I decided to offer something that built on the foundation of my previous work on American–East Asian relations, primarily *state-to-state* relations, and to go further in the direction in which Akira Iriye had been pushing me over the years: to look more closely at American–East Asian *cultural* relations. The focus of the lectures was therefore the intensified contact between Americans and the peoples of East Asia during the twentieth century and how this affected their respective cultures.

My thanks go to Ezra Vogel and his colleagues at the Fairbank Center for East Asian Research at Harvard for inviting me to present the Reischauer Lectures; to Liz Perry, Bill Kirby, and Paul Cohen for their generous introductions and hospitality; and to Gordon Chang, Paul Cohen, John Jeffries, Rod MacFarquhar, and Nancy Bernkopf Tucker for their advice on revising the lectures for publication—something I did most grudgingly.

CONTENTS

INTRODUCTION

In December 1968, in his presidential address to the American Historical Association (AHA), the great Harvard sinologist John King Fairbank urged his audience to take up the study of American–East Asian relations as the historian's "Assignment for the '70s." The AHA created a prestigious Committee on American–East Asian Relations, chaired by Ernest R. May and including such luminaries as Fairbank, Arthur Schlesinger, Jr., Oscar Handlin, and Dorothy Borg. The Ford Foundation provided the initial funding to stimulate the study of Asian languages and research in this newly defined field. I was one of those who responded to the call: I wrote the first edition of my history of Chinese-American relations (*America's Response to China*, 1971) during the 1969–70 academic year.

The year of Fairbank's presidential address was also the year of Hanoi's Tet offensive and the massive protests against America's tragic war in Vietnam. Underlying Fairbank's

argument and the AHA's decision to establish the new committee was the assumption that a greater understanding of
the interaction between the United States and East Asia
might spare the peoples on both sides of the Pacific from future mistakes of the kind that led the United States to plunge
into the quagmire in Indochina.

Thirty-one years later, in December 1999, the *Journal of
American History,* the preeminent publication of the Organization of American Historians, devoted an entire issue to
transnational history. One author, an Australian, cited a
famous 1891 essay, "The Significance of History," in which
Frederick Jackson Turner asked: how shall we understand
American history without understanding European history?
Not a single author saw fit to suggest that *East Asia,* north or
south, had an impact on American history—or vice versa.

Having spent most of my adult life writing about American–East Asian relations, I was frustrated by this evidence
that such a narrow view of American history persisted thirty-
one years after Fairbank's presidential address and a quarter
of a century after America's defeat in Vietnam. American civilization is unquestionably more than an extension of European civilization. A generation ago we realized that we had
neglected Africa's contribution to American culture. Surely
the time has come to acknowledge that to understand the
history of the United States, it is also essential to understand
its interaction with East Asia. And certainly the obverse is
also manifest: the cultures of other societies have been

affected by contact with the United States, and this is true for much of East Asia in the twentieth century. The history of East Asia cannot be understood without recognizing the impact of the United States.

In the pages that follow, I will approach the story of this interaction from three discrete angles. First, and most obvious, is the realm of international politics, the collisions of nation-states and empires that stimulate cultural change. I begin by reviewing the role of the United States in East Asia from the closing years of the nineteenth century to the conclusion of the twentieth, noting its growing power and influence in the region. Playing with counterfactuals, I offer some suggestions as to how differently East Asia might have fared had the Americans not been so active. What might have happened to the Philippines had the United States not seized them in 1898? What would the map of East Asia look like today if the Americans had abandoned the region to the Japanese in 1941? What form of government and what kind of society would Japan have developed without the American occupation? How different would the history of Korea have been without American intervention in 1950? What kind of life would the people of Vietnam have in the year 2000 if the Yankees had stayed home?

The focus of my second chapter is the often disparaged "Americanization" of East Asian culture. I examine the ways in which contact with the United States has changed the way East Asian peoples are governed, how they eat, how they think, how they amuse themselves. I look at cultural change, cultural transfer, and the concept of cultural imperialism. The most difficult part of this investigation was separating *American* cultural influence from generic *Western* influence. I have tried to focus specifically on the former, noting that for much of East Asia, globalization has a distinctly American flavor; that for many Asians, the United States is perceived as the center of the world. It appears that Americanization has been most successful and will be most enduring in those instances when coercion was minimal, when Asian peoples freely chose elements of American culture that they perceived as improvements over what their native cultures offered.

My third topic of investigation is the extraordinary "Asianization" of America–the accelerating influence of East Asia on American life and identity, a phenomenon neglected by most students of American history. It is clear that art, film, food, and religion in the United States have been profoundly affected by contact with Asia. In a few years there will be more Buddhists than Jews in the United States, and one in ten Americans will be of Asian ancestry. Of greatest importance is the fact that Asians, especially as a result of the migration waves of the last third of the twentieth century, are changing American identity—what it is to be an American. Finally, to complete the circle, Asian Americans are beginning to affect the course of state-to-state relations.

1

THE STRUGGLE FOR DOMINANCE IN EAST ASIA

At the close of the nineteenth century, the United States and Japan were admitted to membership in the society of "civilized" nations. Gerrit Gong, in his book *The Standard of "Civilization" in International Society*,[1] makes much of the way that standard of civilized behavior, as defined by *Europeans*, was codified in the international law of the day. The reality, of course, is that both countries muscled their way into the club—Japan by defeating China in 1895 and the Americans by destroying the Spanish empire, in East Asia as well as the Caribbean, in 1898. Any remaining reservations about how "civilized" Japan was were dropped when the Japanese defeated the Russians in 1905. There can be no doubt that respect for the law, domestic and international, and adherence to the norms of international behavior were important to European statesmen, but power was the ultimate trump card.

For the first forty-four years of the twentieth century, until its navy was decimated in the battle of Leyte Gulf in October

1944, Japan was the dominant power in East Asia. It faced only sporadic and ineffectual challenges from the United States—until the aftermath of its attack on the American fleet at Pearl Harbor. No European power, with the early and unfortunate exception of Tsarist Russia, was secure enough in Europe or perceived its interests in East Asia sufficiently threatened—or had leaders stupid enough—to risk confrontation with the Japanese. The British were quick to recognize Japan's strength and attempted to secure their interests in the region by entering into an alliance with the Japanese in 1902.

On the sidelines, the Americans, led by men who were unquestionably "Atlanticists," focused on Europe whenever they looked abroad. To them, it was apparent that Europe was the locus of power in the world, whether economic, military, or political. Nonetheless, reflecting the influence of the navalist Alfred T. Mahan, they slowly built up U.S. might in the Pacific, enlarging their Pacific fleet and developing their bases in Hawaii and the Philippines. Armchair strategists such as Brooks Adams stressed the future importance of Asia in world affairs, and a few businessmen salivated over the opportunities of the mythical "China Market." All concluded that it was essential for the United States to control the sea lanes of the North Pacific.

In the last years of the nineteenth century, the American seizure of Hawaii and the Philippines thwarted Japanese ambitions toward both sets of islands. In the Philippines, the

Americans also put an end to peaceful *Chinese* expansion. The Chinese had been migrating to the Philippines for centuries (many, if not most, of the contemporary Filipino elite have Chinese ancestry). When the Philippines were annexed by the United States, the islands became American territory, to which the laws excluding Chinese from the United States applied. When the outraged Chinese minister to the United States, Wu Tingfang, asked if this meant that wherever Americans in their wisdom chose to expand, Chinese would be denied access, the American secretary of state, John Hay, confirmed Wu's apprehensions. The Chinese also faired poorly in 1900 when American troops stationed in the Philippines were available to join the forces of other ostensibly "civilized" nations in crushing the Boxers, who were attempting to rid China of foreign influence. Americans were thus able to join in the looting of Beijing that followed the success in lifting the siege of the diplomatic quarter, bringing much fine art— and some not so fine—back to the United States.

The Philippines might have been better off without the American occupation, but perhaps not. Certainly the culture of the islands would have developed very differently. Most likely, the Japanese would have seized control of the islands. At a minimum, we would have been counting Imelda Marcos's kimonos instead of the huge cache of designer shoes discovered when "People Power" and Cory Aquino overthrew her husband's dictatorship in 1986. Japanese rather than English would likely be the lingua franca of the islands.

And surely Filipinos would not constitute the second largest group of Asian Americans.

Although the Americans preempted Japan's expansion in the Pacific and limited the peaceful expansion of Japanese through migration to the United States and its possessions, they revealed respect for Japanese power by acquiescing, however grudgingly, in Japanese imperialism on the Asian continent. In 1905 Horace Allen, American minister to Korea, begged President Theodore Roosevelt to protect Korean independence, but Roosevelt was convinced for the moment that American interests were served by Japanese expansion, an obstacle to that of the Russians he despised. Subsequently, he fretted over Japan's advantage as the only Great Power privileged to focus exclusively on the affairs of East Asia, unconcerned by the European affairs that held the attention of the United States as well as the other Great Powers. To avoid conflict with Japan over California's treatment of Japanese migrants and to protect Hawaii, Alaska, and the Philippines (which he had come to view as America's "Achilles' heel"), Roosevelt readily appeased the Japanese appetite for continental expansion. When his successor, William Howard Taft, attempted in 1911 to counter Japanese (and Russian) control of Manchuria with a hopeless scheme to have American investors buy into the railroad network in those Chinese provinces, Roosevelt was quick to condemn the effort. He insisted that it was suicidal for the United States to challenge the Japanese, that America lacked the military strength to oppose Japan on the Asian mainland. In brief, while American missionaries in Korea were providing support and havens for Korean nationalists and a handful of Korean nationalists established a military training camp in Nebraska, no American government challenged the Japanese annexation of Korea or criticized the later mistreatment of Koreans.

Throughout the first two decades of the twentieth century, U.S. Department of State specialists in Chinese affairs begged their leaders to stop Japanese inroads into Chinese territory and sovereignty, primarily with regard to Manchuria. They were appalled especially by Japan's effort to make China a virtual Japanese colony with the notorious "Twenty-one Demands" of 1915. Although several efforts to restrain the Japanese were launched by Presidents Taft and Woodrow Wilson, they all failed miserably. Japan was too strong, American interests too minor, and Northeast Asia was left to the Japanese. In the 1920s, when the Japanese pursued their interests more subtly, generally avoiding the use of force, cooperation with Japan was relatively easy. This was the period in which Shidehara Kijuro managed Japanese diplomacy, the era Akira Iriye has labeled "After Imperialism,"[2] suggesting that Shidehara and his colleagues were responsive to Anglo-American complaints about Japanese behavior in China.

In 1931 and 1932, however, anger erupted in the United States, as elsewhere in the world, over Japanese aggression in Manchuria and the Japanese military's disruption of the peace machinery created in the 1920s. Supporters of the popular and influential American peace movement were devastated by Japan's blatant violation of the Covenant of the League of Nations, of the obligation to respect China's sovereignty and territorial integrity which it had undertaken during the Washington Conference of 1921–1922, and of the commitment Japan had incurred when its representative signed the Paris Peace Pact ("Kellogg-Briand Pact") of 1928, perceived by many as outlawing war. But the Manchurian crisis could not long hold the attention of Americans struggling desperately to survive the Great Depression. Had Bill Clinton's political bulldog James Carville been around then, he doubtless would have said, "It's the economy, stupid."

No event anywhere in the world could compete for very long with the depression for Franklin Delano Roosevelt's attention—certainly not before 1937, when full-scale war began in China. Until then—and for more than a year afterward—FDR's policy, like that of his Uncle Teddy, stressed avoidance of conflict with Japan. Much as he disliked what the Japanese were doing in China, Roosevelt, when he could look beyond domestic affairs, was unquestionably more concerned with events in Europe such as the Spanish Civil War and the menacing actions of Nazi Germany. He managed to provide small-scale aid to the Chinese over the next few years, but when war came to Europe he concentrated his country's efforts on aid to Great Britain. Increasingly after the fall of France in 1940, the United States was engaged in the war against Hitler, initially as a non-belligerent and in an undeclared naval war in the autumn of 1941.

The war in Asia was a distraction, a war in which the United States perceived no vital interest, a war in which Roosevelt hoped to avoid involvement. Nonetheless, the United States began applying economic sanctions against Japan in 1940 and intensified them in 1941, ultimately rejecting a proposed modus vivendi with Japan and provoking the attack on Pearl Harbor. The reasoning behind Roosevelt's policies toward Japan in those crucial years is probably less well understood than any other major policy decision in the history of America's foreign relations.

The United States had not chosen to antagonize Japan as part of a plan to replace Japan as the dominant power in East Asia. Indeed, concern for China, for East Asia per se, had relatively little to do with the pressure the United States exerted on Japan. Neither the famed Open Door notes of 1899 and 1900 urging the preservation of China's independence and territorial integrity nor lust for the China market drove American policy. As historians such as Dorothy Borg and Waldo Heinrichs have demonstrated, it was Japan's alliance with Hitler's Germany that was critical in determining the American response.[3] Aid to China was designed to keep the Chinese in the war, keeping the Japanese engaged so that they would be unable to put pressure on the British empire or to undermine British efforts in Europe and North Africa. In the autumn of 1941, the principal concern of Roosevelt and Churchill was preventing a Japanese attack on the Soviet Union at a moment when the Germans were knocking at Stalin's door. The result was a war in Asia which Roosevelt did not want and which several able scholars, such as Paul W. Schroeder and Bruce M. Russett, have argued was unnecessary.[4]

In that war, the United States destroyed the Japanese empire, which had come to encompass virtually all of East Asia, north and south. And unhesitatingly, the United States moved to establish itself as the dominant power in the region, seeking to transform the Pacific into what John Dower once called an "American lake," and establishing what Bruce Cumings and Chalmers Johnson see as American hegemony over East Asia.[5] Obviously, had the United States succeeded in staying out of the war in Asia, East Asia would look very different today. It is, to be sure, unlikely that the Japanese would still control their Greater East Asian Coprosperity Sphere—that they would have been any more successful than European imperialists in suppressing resistance and liberation movements in every country in the region. Nonetheless, imagining an extended Japanese occupation of China and Southeast Asia—remembering the brutality with which they treated Chinese everywhere, recalling the persistent savagery of the Japanese military police, the notorious *kenpeitai,* in all of the areas they controlled—suggests the relatively benign effects of substituting American for Japanese dominance.

In 1945, the principal American goal in East Asia was control of Japan and of as many Pacific islands as could be seized and either developed as bases in the future or denied to a potential enemy. The U.S. government had little interest in Southeast Asia other than in the Philippines, which had been promised and would be granted independence. It should be noted, however, that the Americans intended to retain their major naval and air bases in the islands. Interest in the Asian mainland was minimal, despite unease within the American military about Soviet intentions in Northeast Asia, specifically the disposition of Soviet forces that had overrun the Japanese in Manchuria and northern Korea.

Control of Japan was the major prize, simultaneously giving the United States access to a vast range of air and naval bases and enabling it to restrain the region's only conceivable threat to American security. The United States shared neither bases nor responsibility for the occupation of Japan with its erstwhile allies—certainly not with the Chinese, who arguably had suffered most at Japanese hands, not with the Soviets, who were behaving badly in Eastern Europe, and not with the British, Australians, New Zealanders, or anyone else. There would be no future threat to peace in the Pacific. The Yanks had come, and they would keep the peace. Clearly, American leaders could not imagine a threat emanating from China. Perhaps this was racist contempt for the Chinese, but more likely the estimate of Chinese power was based primarily on the unhappy experiences the American military had working with Jiang Jieshi (Chiang Kai-shek) during the war, the perception of Chinese troops badly led and unwilling to fight.[6]

The evolution of the Cold War in the late 1940s shook American complacency about East Asia. Unquestionably, Europe was the central arena in the confrontation between the United States and the Soviet Union. The architects of victory in World War II, men such as George C. Marshall and Dean Acheson, were still directing policy, and they reflexively continued their Europe-first strategy. Events in China and Korea, however, forced them to look across the Pacific.

The Chinese civil war was the first major crisis in Asia. Most Americans who had worked with Jiang during World War II despised him. They had no faith in his ability to lead China and no illusions that he would create the liberal democracy they hoped to see emerge in China—and everywhere else. But they feared that the Chinese Communists would be a front for Soviet imperialism. Throughout the war and in the months immediately following the Japanese surrender, American diplomats attempted to mediate between Jiang's Guomindang and Mao's Communists, to prevent civil war. At the same time, Washington continued to recognize Jiang's government as the government of China and to aid its efforts to reestablish its authority over Japanese-occupied territory. When mediation failed, the United States, albeit grudgingly and sparingly, supported the Guomindang against the Communists. Uncertain of Stalin's intentions in Northeast Asia—or elsewhere—Americans hoped Jiang could keep China from coming under Soviet control.

When it became clear in 1946 that the Soviets were withdrawing their troops from Manchuria and had no intention of moving into North China, American concern diminished. A communist victory in China would be unfortunate, but not catastrophic. China was weak and could not pose a threat to the United States. Patriotism seemed intense among members of the Chinese Communist Party. A communist China would not likely become a Soviet puppet.

As it became evident late in 1948 that Mao Zedong's forces would win the struggle for control of China, Acheson decided to seek accommodation with the Communists as a means of keeping China from becoming a Soviet ally. He and his associates were discouraged by the signing of the Sino-Soviet alliance early in 1950, but the Americans, aware of the hard bargain Stalin had driven, remained hopeful of being able to drive a wedge between them. The deal between Washington and Beijing that Acheson envisioned was still on the table when war broke out in Korea in June 1950.

As part of the arrangement that the United States was prepared to offer the People's Republic of China, American leaders signaled their willingness to abandon Taiwan, the island to which Jiang's rump regime had fled after its defeat on the mainland. Acheson and his president, Harry S Truman, gave speeches preparing the public for the Communist conquest of the island, which was expected in the summer of 1950. In this manner the American government publicly and explicitly declared that its defensive perimeter, encompassing the area that it perceived as vital to its security, did not include Taiwan or any part of the Asian mainland. Asked specifically what would happen if Communist-controlled North Korea invaded the non-Communist South, Acheson replied that the South Koreans would have to defend themselves or, failing that, appeal to the United Nations.

Soviet and Chinese documents obtained in the 1990s suggest that the defensive perimeter speech, combined with the earlier withdrawal of American military forces from Korea and the subsequent refusal of the American Congress to appropriate funds to enable South Korea to defend itself, persuaded Stalin that the Yanks were not coming. He could yield to the North Korean leader Kim Il Sung's pleas for permission to attack—and for the offensive equipment necessary to succeed.

Stalin gambled—and he lost. His failed gamble changed the nature of the Cold War. The Americans reversed their policy, sent troops to Korea, stopped the Soviet-directed North Korean advance short of victory, and in three months smashed the North Korean army. They had repelled aggression, demonstrated the credibility of the United Nations, and sent a message to Stalin that the United States was not to be trifled with. But then came that classic case of "mission creep," of war aims expanded when victory comes too easily.

American leaders decided to send U.N. forces under the command of the American general Douglas MacArthur across the thirty-eighth parallel dividing North from South Korea, in order to create a unified, non-Communist, conceivably democratic Korea. U.N. troops moved north despite Chinese warnings and encountered hundreds of thousands of Chinese troops—who drove them all the way back down the peninsula and almost off of it.

Eventually the Americans, the South Koreans, and their U.N. allies stopped the Chinese offensive and stabilized the battlefield where it all started, at the thirty-eighth parallel. But the truce came only after millions of Koreans, hundreds of thousands of Chinese, and more than fifty thousand American and other U.N. troops had lost their lives. Blood, lots of it, had been shed on both sides—and the arms race began in earnest. Hopes for a Chinese-American accommodation were shelved indefinitely. Although the United States refused Jiang's offer to send troops to Korea, Washington resumed aid to Jiang's forces, gave covert support to their operations against the mainland, and placed elements of the U.S. Navy in the Taiwan Strait. Taiwan, like South Korea, was no longer outside the defensive perimeter of the United States. It was no longer unprotected, susceptible to attack at a moment of Mao's choosing. China and the United States had become enemies, and Jiang was the principal beneficiary.

There are reputable scholars who contend that the United States should not have intervened in what they perceive as a

Korean civil war.[7] In general, their argument that the southern regime of Syngman Rhee was reprehensible, that it acted provocatively toward the north, and that the United States prevented the reunification of Korea is beyond dispute. Similarly, they are unquestionably correct in their insistence that the initiative for the attack came from Kim Il Sung, not Stalin. On the other hand, they tend to understate the Soviet role and the threat that a united Korea allied to the Soviet Union posed to American friends and interests in the region.

Certainly American intervention had an enormous impact on East Asia. After preparing to abandon Taiwan to the Chinese Communists in late 1949 and early 1950, the United States resumed its support for Jiang's regime and reinvolved itself in China's civil war. Fifty years later, as Americans wait anxiously to see if they will be drawn into a war in defense of Taiwan's autonomy, it is fascinating to recall how close they came to having the issue resolved in 1950, or more likely 1951. Had it not been for the Korean War, the People's Liberation Army would have invaded Taiwan in 1951 and probably would have conquered the island with relative ease in the absence of American intervention. And resolving the Chinese civil war in that manner would have precluded the emergence of democracy on Taiwan in our lifetime.

More obviously, the history of Korea would have been very different. About thirty years ago, the president of a Korean university at which I spoke, a former general, invited me to his home for lunch. He then informed me that the Americans had done something to Koreans that not even the Japanese had done: they had divided his country. I noted that in 1950 the United States had had the opportunity to allow Korea to be reunited and asked if that would have been his preference. (Lunch was terminated abruptly. I was not offered dessert.) In the 1980s, South Korean students were insisting that the United States had crushed a nationalist struggle for reunification. Again, a sobering counterfactual: if the Americans had stayed home in 1950, what would Korea be like today, presumably with Kim Jong Il and his colleagues in control of a united Korea? The economic "miracle on the Han" likely would not have occurred, and democracy would still be light-years away for the people of South Korea. And there would be far fewer Koreans living in the United States. Would Japan have continued to abide by its "peace" constitution? Would it have refrained from becoming a nuclear power? I cannot answer any of these questions with certainty, but no one can doubt the enormous impact of American intervention and the subsequent American military build-up in the Pacific on the power relationships of the states of the region.

The picture for the remaining years of the Cold War was not a pretty one. Once East Asia was perceived as a major arena in the struggle between the Soviet Union and the United States, American leaders were determined to dominate the entire area, including Southeast Asia, militarily. Many of us would consider America's role in Southeast Asia indefensible. Sadly, for all the misery inflicted on the peoples of that region, it is difficult to make a case for the salience of American intervention.

In Northeast Asia, the story is quite different. As the United States extended its alliance system to East Asia, attempting to contain communist influence there, as in Europe, it provided South Korea and Taiwan with support that was absolutely essential for the survival of those two countries. Some might argue that their governments were not worth saving—and there was a time when I might have agreed. But looking back today, I have no regrets. Both South Korea and Taiwan have emerged as democracies in which their people enjoy freedom and prosperity, far greater than they would have known if abandoned to their communist rivals. And, of course, the United States was also protecting Japan, enabling the Japanese to prosper in a relatively secure environment since World War II.

Less happily, in the 1950s, the American government became obsessed with a perceived need to stop the expansion of communism in Southeast Asia. French imperialism in Indochina had been redefined by 1950 as part of the struggle against communism. Although France's defeat by the forces of Ho Chi Minh was unquestionably regretted in Washington, it did provide what American leaders perceived as the opportunity for the United States to step in and do the job right, to do what the French lacked the strength or will to do.

The Southeast Asia Treaty Organization (SEATO) was created in 1954 to provide reassurance to some of the region's states. Thailand was given the promise of support its leaders craved, and Vietnam, Laos, and Cambodia received a hint of comparable support. South Vietnam became an American protectorate as the power of the United States replaced that of France in Indochina.

A recalcitrant Indonesia, determined to remain neutral in the Cold War, was viewed in Washington as tilting toward Moscow and Beijing. Its president, Sukarno, had emerged as a leader in the "nonaligned" camp, but American leaders feared he was becoming a pawn of the Indonesian Communist party. As he struggled against separatist movements in Sumatra and Celebes in 1957, the United States decided to aid the insurgents. Initially, the Americans supplied arms and training to rebel forces and then sent unmarked bombers. By 1958 the United States was preparing to intervene openly to support anti-communist forces in Indonesia. The Americans hoped to destabilize the country and get rid of Sukarno. Contrary to American expectations, the rebellion was crushed by the Indonesian military and before long, with perhaps unseemly haste, the United States was competing with the Soviet bloc to supply weapons to the Indonesian army. The leaders in Washington, left with few alternatives, could only hope that the Indonesian generals would contain communism in their country.

By the late 1950s, the United States had become the dominant power in Southeast Asia, a region in which it had shown little interest prior to the Korean War. None of its allies had the strength to protect the region, and with the withdrawal of European power, American leaders discerned a vacuum that could not be left to be filled by the Chinese Communists. Even John Fairbank, the leading China scholar in America, wrote in 1966 in the midst of his campaign to integrate China into the world community that Beijing's subversive efforts to foment wars of national liberation had to be countered, that a line had to be drawn in Vietnam to prevent the further expansion of Chinese communism.[8] And Edwin Reischauer, Harvard's great Japanologist, on leave to serve as his country's ambassador to Japan, became convinced that communist expansion in Southeast Asia threatened Japan's trading lifelines and ultimately its security, and thus he supported America's war in Vietnam.

The effort to create a viable non-communist state in southern Vietnam demonstrated the limits as well as the arrogance of American power. The communist leaders of northern Vietnam refused to surrender half their nation and, with Chinese and Soviet assistance, they prevailed. They would have won the battle to unify their country by 1965 had the United States not sent hundreds of thousands of troops to prop up the tottering Saigon regime. Inevitably, however, the Americans tired of the war and went home, abandoning most of their surrogates. Vietnam has fared poorly under communist rule since 1975, but the misery inflicted on its people by the American effort to divide the country may well have been greater. I know of no calculus adequate to measure the pain endured by the Vietnamese people.

In his multivolume *International History of the War in Vietnam,* R. B. Smith argued that the United States was fighting in Vietnam to save Indonesia.[9] If so, the defeat in Vietnam, the loss of American influence in Indochina, mattered little. Until 1965, Sukarno, encouraged by the Soviet Union, continued to irritate the leaders in Washington (and in London, the Hague, and much of Southeast Asia as well). In 1965 he withdrew Indonesia from the United Nations, apparently aligning himself with Mao Zedong in opposition to that organization. The coup that followed, resulting in one of the worst massacres in world history, had—from an American perspective—the salutary effect of pushing Sukarno aside and bringing to power one General Suharto, who eliminated the communist menace and facilitated a striking growth of American influence in the islands.

Despite its defeat in Vietnam, the United States remained the dominant power in East Asia, north and south, underlining the absurdity of the overblown rhetoric about the dire consequences that would follow a communist victory in Vietnam. In 1975, after the war in Vietnam ended, there remained no threat to American preeminence anywhere in the region. The defensive perimeter of 1949–1950 had been extended to include Taiwan and South Korea, and no nation dared move against it. By then, too, the United States had been edging toward a tacit alliance with China against the Soviet Union, as evidenced by some of the recently declassified transcripts of conversations between Henry Kissinger and Zhou Enlai in the early 1970s.[10]

Relations between the United States and China generally have been perceived in Washington since 1950 as increasingly important. Fears of a resurgent Japanese militarism faded quickly even before the end of the occupation. Indeed, successive American administrations regretted the peace constitution imposed on Japan by the occupation authorities and lobbied in Tokyo for an increased Japanese military role in Asia. Perhaps fortunately for all concerned, most Japanese leaders showed little interest. But China, as a Soviet surrogate in the region, worried the United States. It was perceived as a threat to the American position in Korea and Southeast Asia, especially after its success against American forces in Korea and its support for the Vietnamese against France in the early 1950s.

American efforts to isolate and undermine the Beijing regime in the 1950s failed. Overtures to Washington from the People's Republic in the 1950s, similar to the terms Kissinger and President Richard Nixon accepted in the 1970s, were rejected. Crises in 1954–1955 and 1958 in the Taiwan Strait increased tensions briefly, but the U.S. government moved slowly toward acceptance of the fact that the Communist Party would retain control of China for the foreseeable future. In due course American leaders concluded that the Chinese would be less dangerous if they were integrated into the international community. A policy labeled "containment without isolation" gradually took shape.

Eisenhower spoke publicly of the foolishness of trade sanctions against China and facilitated the broadening of British and Japanese trade with the People's Republic—although domestic political restraints and opposition to his views within his administration prevented direct trade between the United States and China.[11] As the historian Nancy Bernkopf Tucker has demonstrated, even John Foster Dulles toyed with a "two Chinas" policy. In my own research for a book about Dean Rusk, I was astonished to find Dulles and Rusk working together toward that end in the mid-1950s.[12]

Some ground was lost in the 1960s because of John F. Kennedy's slim grip on power and his obsession with the imagined threat from China. Despite everything his brilliant National Security Council adviser on Chinese affairs (and subsequently Harvard professor of American–East Asian relations), James C. Thomson, tried to teach him, he was slow to understand the significance of the Sino-Soviet split. In mitigation, it should be remembered that leading scholars like Tang Tsou were insisting that the split was simply a disagreement as to how to destroy the United States. Intensification of the American effort in Vietnam was justified by the view that Hanoi was an extension of Chinese power, and of course the People's Republic did aid Hanoi substantially with men and materiel.[13] Fear of the Chinese challenge soared when they succeeded in testing an atomic bomb in 1964. As Dean Rusk was wont to say, the United States was about to confront "a billion Chinese armed with nuclear weapons." And then there was the Great Proletarian Cultural Revolution, with its terrifying evidence of Mao's irrationality.

Nonetheless, the United States struggled toward some sort of modus vivendi with Beijing. Assistant Secretary of State Roger Hilsman publicly floated a doomed "two Chinas" policy early in the presidency of Lyndon Johnson. "Containment without isolation" became the phrase of choice in 1966 after televised hearings on policy toward China presided over by the chairman of the Senate Committee on Foreign Relations, J. William Fulbright. But Mao was not yet interested. It required an assist from the Soviets to drive China and the United States together.

Soviet bloc intervention in Czechoslovakia in 1968, to crush a communist government that was encouraging political pluralism, worried Mao and his colleagues. Moscow justified its action with the Brezhnev Doctrine, claiming the right to intervene in any socialist state in which Moscow determined that socialism was in danger. The doctrine was manifestly an implied threat to the People's Republic of China. The Soviets had positioned half a million soldiers on China's borders and expressed contempt for Mao's vision of socialism. In 1969, the two communist states were involved in border incidents in which Chinese and Soviet troops exchanged fire. Mao was persuaded it was time to play the American card, and two years later Kissinger showed up in Beijing.

Both the United States and China were suddenly eager to bolster each other's power in East Asia in the hope of intimidating the Soviet Union. The rapprochement they achieved in the early 1970s, following the earlier Sino-Soviet split, constituted the single most important shift in the balance of power in the history of the Cold War. The Soviet Union's one-time ally was now working with the United States against the Soviet Union. China was no longer threatened by the United States. The United States was no longer fearful of a Chinese challenge to America's place in East Asia. (All was well so long as the question of Taiwan was kept off the table.) The United States even enjoyed the luxury of focusing on its foreign economic problems, evidenced by its mounting pressures on Japan to solve the American balance-of-payments problem.

Obviously, the decline and ultimate collapse of the Soviet Union in the 1980s had enormous ramifications for Europe. Its impact on East Asia was less immediately apparent, but its importance gradually became clear. Vietnam and North Korea were left without a patron, and China's security was no longer threatened. Shortly after "normalizing" relations with the United States, in 1979 Beijing had sent troops into Vietnam to punish the Vietnamese for invading Cambodia and for aligning themselves with the Soviets in opposition to China. It was clear that with their new American connection, the Chinese no longer feared the Soviets. But, not surprisingly, as fear of the Soviet Union receded in China, relations with the United States began to fray.

The critical irritant in the Chinese-American relationship was—and remains—Taiwan. In extremis in the early 1970s, the Chinese had agreed to postpone resolution of the Taiwan question. The issue was papered over in the Shanghai Communiqué of 1972, but it is clear from transcripts of the talks Kissinger and Nixon had with Mao and Zhou that the Chinese had been led to believe that the United States accepted their "one China" formula and would abandon the Republic of China on Taiwan.[14] Nixon and Kissinger professed to believe, quite reasonably, that in the short run Taiwan could protect itself. In the long run, they hoped a peaceful solution could be found. Of course, "in the long run," much like the "decent interval" they sought before the collapse of the Saigon government, they would be out of office and responsibility for failure could be placed on the shoulders of a future administration (preferably, for Nixon, a Democratic one headed by Senator Ted Kennedy, the most prominent remaining member of the family for which he had developed an obsessive hatred).

As the Taiwan issue festered in the years that followed, aggravated by the Taiwan Relations Act in which the U.S. Congress inserted a clause committing the Americans to make available to Taiwan whatever it needed to defend itself, China began to back away from the United States. President

Ronald Reagan's outspoken support for Taiwan left the men in Beijing less confident of the value of their strategic relationship with the United States, especially as the Soviets lost strength and the Americans gained. Chinese leaders became uncertain that American power in East Asia would be an asset to them. Increasingly mistrustful of the intentions of the United States toward Taiwan, they were less accepting of the dominance of the region by the Americans, even if it was largely offshore.

The hostile American response to the June 1989 Tiananmen massacre, when the Chinese government sent the People's Liberation Army to crush its citizens who were demonstrating for an end to the Communist Party's arbitrary exercise of power, angered Beijing. The rapid imposition of sanctions against China by Washington forced the Chinese to recognize that with the end of the Cold War, the United States was less likely to ignore human rights violations; that in the absence of a strategic imperative, the focus on ideological differences was likely to sharpen. China's modernization program was (and remains) partly dependent on access to the U.S. market and American technology. A rupture in Chinese-American relations clearly would not be in China's interest, but the leaders of the Chinese Communist Party were not willing to commit suicide to facilitate economic growth. They would not yield to American pressures if to do so might jeopardize their power. Of course, they quickly realized that their allies in the American business community were too eager for trade and investment opportunities in China to allow the United States to sever relations or to maintain sanctions for very long. They would wait for the Americans to lift the sanctions. As Deng Xiaoping told his American interlocutors, "he who tied the knot must untie it."[15] And the Americans blinked first.

In the 1990s, the Chinese demonstrated increasing dissatisfaction with the existing power balance in East Asia and demanded a greater role for themselves. They did not hesitate to display their military might around the South China Sea, paying little heed to the claims of several Southeast Asian states to some of the islands and offshore resources of those waters. They left no doubt of their perception of their importance to efforts to prevent war on the Korean peninsula, where they occasionally attempted to impart wisdom to the Pyongyang government while deepening their relationship with Seoul. Most of all, they wanted an end to American dominance—and a free hand with Taiwan.

The United States, on the other hand, was quite comfortable with the existing power relationships and apprehensive about Chinese intentions. Occasionally, the Americans were insensitive to the Chinese desire to be respected as a Great Power in arenas like the United Nations. The Chinese were shaken by the handling of the Kosovo question in 1999, when the United States bypassed the Security Council, where China opposed the use of force against Slobodan Milosevic's Serbia, and used NATO's military power to serve its purpose.

Not without reason, Chinese strategists concluded that the United States will not share power with China voluntarily. And, of course, the Chinese were outraged by the American destruction of their embassy in Belgrade, never convinced that it had been inadvertent.

At the beginning of the twenty-first century, the challenge to the international political order in East Asia clearly comes from China. It is unwilling to accept continued American dominance in the region, and the United States is unwilling to surrender that position. The U.S. military recognizes the rise of Chinese power and influence, and its planners see East Asia as the most likely arena for the next conflict.[16] They perceive Great Power competition and the locus of economic power shifting toward Asia. The U.S. Navy has begun to transfer forces, specifically attack submarines, from the Atlantic to the Pacific. Most American policymakers probably remain "Atlanticists," but Eurocentrism is fading rapidly.

At the end of the "American century" in East Asia, some of the questions we face are the following: Will China develop the capability to challenge the United States in the foreseeable future, or is it more likely to implode, as suggested by several of the essays in a volume recently edited by Merle Goldman and Roderick MacFarquhar?[17] Can the United States and China find mutually acceptable roles in the region, sparing their peoples a new Cold War or military confrontation? And, lest we forget, there is another major nation in

East Asia—Japan—with its own aspirations for a greater role in regional and world affairs.[18]

These, of course, are questions for the future, for the century just beginning. My argument here is simply that the projection of American power across the Pacific, into East Asia, had an enormous impact on the history of that region in the twentieth century. Obviously, I cannot offer counterfactuals with certainty, but I want to end this chapter with one contentious argument: despite the horrors of Vietnam, of Hiroshima and Nagasaki, of the brutality of the suppression of the Filipino fight for independence, and a myriad of other, lesser American transgressions, most people in East Asia are far better off today than they would have been if the Americans had stayed home.

Winston Churchill once argued that flawed as democracy may be, it is the best form of government known to man. Democracy in Japan, South Korea, and Taiwan, flawed as it may be, has provided the people of those countries with a far better life than most of their ancestors knew—and they would not likely enjoy that life, its freedom and prosperity, without the role the United States played in their history. Whatever hope the people of the rest of East Asia have of enjoying the universal rights promised by the United Nations, the provision of which is a condition of membership in the society of civilized nations at the beginning of the twenty-first century, can be attributed to the power of the United States. Americans enabled most of their countries to liberate themselves from the brutality of Japanese imperialism and contributed to relieving some of them of the burdens placed upon them by communist ideologues. And America, despite all the faults of which we who live in it are aware, remains a beacon of liberty and prosperity to the people of East Asia, as to much of the rest of the world.

2

THE AMERICANIZATION
OF EAST ASIA

All students of East Asia have confronted the phenomenon we once referred to as Asia's "response to the West." We have looked at "Westernization" and "modernization," and more recently at "transnationalism" and "globalization." All of these concepts refer to changes in the societies we study, changes in their culture, generally implying convergence with our own culture, even homogenization, an erosion of the traditional culture that we, as *tourists,* long to see—and that we, as tourists, tend to romanticize.

Obviously, this process antedates the rise of American influence. It is probably only the French who blame all cultural change on "Americanization," on American "cultural imperialism." (France's hysterical fear of American popular culture is epitomized by Marguerite Duras's likening of EuroDisney, in Paris, to a "cultural Chernobyl.")[1] Nonetheless, some of the changes in the way the people of East Asia live today—what they eat and drink, how they play and how they pray, how they are governed and how they dream of being governed—can be blamed on or credited to the United States, its image in their minds and the role the United States has played in their lives.

During the course of the twentieth century, the United States had an impact on popular culture, education, religion, political and economic thought and practices in most countries of East Asia. Little of the Americanization that occurred was forced on Asian peoples. In general, American efforts to *impose* cultural change failed. Instead, Asians chose those elements of American culture that pleased *them*—modifying them, more often than not, to suit local taste, and ultimately indigenizing them. Sometimes they selected cultural artifacts that seemed familiar; sometimes they preferred the exotic, seeking, for a variety of reasons, a radical departure from tradition. There were occasions when the United States might reasonably have been charged with cultural imperialism, cases of deliberate and coercive efforts to reshape nations in its own image, but that does not prove to be a useful concept for understanding most of the cultural transfer that occurred.

The American role in effecting cultural change in East Asia usually has been passive. In most instances there has been no purposeful action by the government of the United States. The most obvious example is when peoples of East Asia accept an image of America. They might perceive America as the freest society in the world, or the United States as the richest or most powerful or most modern country in the world—and seek to emulate it. They try to determine what element in American life produces the desired result and then attempt to replicate it in their own societies.

Similarly, Asian peoples might see aspects of American culture that strike them as more satisfying or entertaining than what their own culture offers. They may enjoy *Dallas* or *Bay Watch* or *Little House on the Prairie* more than the programs produced locally. Every week 300,000 young Japanese, craving a taste of New York night-life, watch Fuji Television's *Soullook: Seize the Night,* broadcast live from the Cheetah Club in Manhattan.[2] Until very recently, the only alternative to government-controlled TV in South Korea was the U.S. Army channel, which offered American programming twenty-four hours a day. It is hardly surprising that young Koreans soaked up American popular culture. In Malaysia, Ian Buruma found that the urban middle class preferred American popular culture to Malay plays (and a Malay playwright friend of his complained that "Malay culture does not exist").[3]

In all of these instances, people act *freely* to take what they please, for their own ends, and adapt it in any way that seems useful to them. Generally, their sense of national identity is not threatened. Certainly, in their own minds, few of them feel less Chinese or Japanese, Korean, Thai, or Vietnamese.

Throughout history, people have struggled to find ways to use alien ideas, alien technology, alien culture to improve their lives. They seek to do so with minimal sacrifice of their own values. Given that the United States was the world's leading power for most of the twentieth century, it is not surprising that American culture is attractive to much of the world—or that some people fear Americanization as a threat to their traditions and their power. To be sure, cultural change is rarely, if ever, without cost. It can be especially painful for more mature, venerable members of a society, who see their experience ignored, their traditions rejected by children and grandchildren enamored of all that is new and different.

Often, however, it is cultural and political *elites* who are most troubled, who attempt to deny their people the right to make choices, who wish to reserve the power to choose which foreign ideas will be adopted. Li Peng, the putative villain of China's Tiananmen massacre, forewarned American visitors that his interest in importing Western science and technology did not extend to importing Western values. Constantly apprehensive about American influence, the Chinese communist government has tried frantically to adhere to the *ti-yung* principle proclaimed during the Qing dynasty a century ago: preserve Chinese culture for essentials; use Western methods to achieve technical progress. This has resulted in campaigns against "bourgeois liberalization" and "spiritual pollution" and Beijing's recent efforts to control the Internet, as China welcomed foreigners, their money, and their technology. Of course, the Chinese are not alone. The other communist states of East Asia are even more restrictive of American and other Western influences, as is Burma. And the leaders of nominally democratic Singapore and Malaysia have enjoyed a degree of notoriety for their strident defense of "Asian values."

Certainly there have also been situations in which elements of American culture were *imposed* upon indigenous peoples, in which the full force of American might, of the American state, was brought to bear. These were situations in which the people's freedom to choose was greatly inhibited, most obviously in the Philippines during the colonial era and in Japan during the occupation. In both instances, the successes and failures of American cultural imperialism may be instructive.

I will focus first on American culture freely chosen. A good place to begin is the American political and social practices that attracted Chinese, Japanese, Korean, and Vietnamese intellectuals in the closing years of the nineteenth century and early years of the twentieth. The historian Akira Iriye has discussed those Japanese who looked to the rise of American power in the late nineteenth century as an example of how to enhance a nation's strength without resorting to imperialism.[4] These men rejected arguments that the European model, gaining wealth and power through the seizure of colonies, was the only path to greatness. The U.S. seizure of the Philippines in 1898 proved disillusioning to them—and they were probably ignorant of what had been done to the American Indians whose territory white Americans coveted, or to the Mexicans. But the point is that they had an *image* of American political culture that they tried to use as a model for their own country.

Carol Gluck has pointed to the admiration some Japanese intellectuals had for the vitality of American life in the early years of the twentieth century, what one saw as the "spirit of a Theodore Roosevelt." Another saw American democracy as an answer to the problem of underemployment of educated Japanese: in America a university graduate allegedly could drive a taxi without shame.[5] The writer Nagai Kafu lived in the United States from 1903 to 1907 and had no illusions about racism there. Mitsuko Iriye notes, however, that contact with American women allowed Kafu to imagine an ideal mate who could be his "social and intellectual equal and still retain her femininity," as opposed to the Japanese "good-wife-and-wise-mother" stereotype—whose husband found life in the pleasure quarters more interesting than at home.[6]

Chinese officials and diplomats visiting the United States in the last decades of the Qing dynasty were tremendously impressed by the level of industrialization they found. Beyond technology, some suspected that American institutions and values contributed to the country's economic progress.

For those who would modernize China, the United States seemed worthy of emulation.[7] Liang Qichao, arguing that destruction of the traditional order was essential for progress, contended that the United States owed its strength to its war for independence and its civil war.[8] Chinese reformers and revolutionaries early in the twentieth century saw the American political system as the appropriate model for a China freed of the Qing dynasty: China, too, would become a republic and Sun Yat-sen would be its George Washington. Sun himself looked to the United States for the form of government he envisioned, and his economic theories were heavily influenced by the American writer Henry George. Ryan Fisk Dunch suggests that some Chinese gained their sense of nationalism and national symbols—flags and patriotic hymns—from American missionaries. He notes that even the Qing's governor-general in Fujian referred in 1910 to the United States as being "at the head of the enlightened nations of the earth." After the revolution of 1911, according to Dunch, Chinese in Fujian, Protestants and non-Christians alike, explicitly pointed to America as a model for the new republic.[9]

The leading Korean reformers at the end of the nineteenth century, So Chae-p'il (Philip Jaisohn) and Yun Ch'i-ho of the Independence Club, had both studied in the United States; So actually became an American citizen before returning to Korea. They learned about the Founding Fathers, the ideals of the constitution, the rights and duties of citizens, and the role of government in a democracy. Striving to create a liberal democracy in Korea, they and many of their followers saw America as the model.[10]

Mark Bradley describes how Vietnamese intellectuals early in the twentieth century imagined that the answers to their people's needs might be found in the American experience and in American political philosophy. Eager to mobilize their countrymen against French imperialism, they idealized the "heroic voluntarism" of the American revolution, of a handful of dedicated men and women fighting successfully to free themselves from the world's most powerful empire. Ho Chi Minh, writing in 1927, argued that the American experience made the United States a valuable model and expressed admiration for the Declaration of Independence. Even as Ho and his colleagues grew more radical, concerned that the American revolution had done too little for workers and peasants, they continued to embrace George Washington, Benjamin Franklin, Patrick Henry, and Abraham Lincoln.[11]

Across East Asia, in China, Japan, Korea, and Indochina, in the early years of the twentieth century, men and women aspiring to lead their people to liberty, prosperity, and greater repute in the modern world looked to the United States as a model. Most perceived America's democratic institutions as the foundation of that nation's emergence as a world power. After World War I, as a result of that war, European civilization was discredited in the minds of many intellectuals in Asia. The United States, however, came out of the war with its power and reputation enhanced. In particular, many people in East Asia were inspired by Woodrow Wilson's Fourteen Points. His call for self-determination for all peoples resonated among those who were victims of imperialism. Stimulated in part by the contrast between the words of the American president and the reality of Japanese colonialism, Koreans took to the streets on March 1, 1919, demanding an end to Japanese rule. Similarly frustrated by the failure of the Paris Peace Conference to validate Wilson's promise by returning control of Shandong province to China, students in Beijing began an anti-Japanese rampage on May 4, 1919. In Paris, Korean intellectuals led by Syngman Rhee, a Princeton Ph.D., and Vietnamese, including Ho Chi Minh, were energized by Wilson's call for self-determination, however little it actually accomplished.

Self-determination for the people of China and Korea did not rank high on any list of Japanese priorities. The government of Japan was well aware of American opposition to Japanese imperialism and acted as necessary to circumvent it. Nonetheless, many Japanese in the 1920s were willing to set aside much of the European culture they had come to admire and open their minds and doors to an imagined American culture. An enormous body of work introducing the United States was published in Japan in the early decades of the twentieth century.

American society was perceived by many Japanese as younger and more dynamic than European societies. Americans were freer (although this is the era in which the scientific management principles of the American "efficiency" expert Frederick Winslow Taylor, hardly a source of worker freedom, caught on in Japanese factories). In the 1920s a Japanese publisher produced a magazine modeled after the popular American *Saturday Evening Post.* Another published a Japanese version of the *Harvard Classics.* They were, as Miriam Silverberg argues, creating a mass culture that "recoded" American institutions and practices for local consumption.[12]

American culture also proved attractive to Chinese who were disillusioned with traditional approaches to political and social problems. Guo Moruo, who was to become a Chinese Communist cultural icon, discovered Walt Whitman's *Leaves of Grass* while studying in Japan, and many of his early poems (1919–1921) reflect Whitman's influence. His biographer, David Roy, contends that it was Whitman who radicalized Guo and facilitated the Chinese writer's ultimate acceptance of Marxist-Leninism.[13] As other Chinese intellectuals searched for a path to modernity, Cai Yuanpei, the leading educator of his time, invited John Dewey to Beijing and introduced him as a "greater thinker than Confucius."[14] And, of course, American-educated Hu Shi, the prominent liberal intellectual of the 1920s, conceived of the modern science and democracy he craved for China in "distinctly Deweyan, not generically Western" terms.[15]

The image of the United States as representative of freedom, wealth, and power grew tremendously after the Second

World War. American mass culture became the rage everywhere. Wherever choice was possible, blue jeans were worn by the young. Coca-Cola was drunk everywhere (except among the Thai and Hmong, who share my preference for Pepsi).[16] Probably forgotten is the outrage of Soviet leader Nikita Khrushchev in the early 1960s at the popularity of Coca-Cola in East Asia, and the absurd Soviet advertising campaign to substitute their sassafras-based Kvass in Japan. Kvass did not catch on with student radicals, who were able to demonstrate against American imperialism in Vietnam without abstaining from Cokes. Several generations of teenagers in Japan used blue jeans and Cokes to demonstrate their alienation from local adult culture, as did their Chinese counterparts when given that option more recently. Perhaps most surprising is the current success of Starbucks coffee among erstwhile tea drinkers in China, Japan, South Korea, Malaysia, the Philippines, Thailand, and Singapore, where shops are "crowded with young white collar workers and trendy teens."[17] The world's busiest Starbucks is in the Shibuya district of Tokyo.

Listening to American music—jazz since the 1920s, later rock and roll and even rap—has proved attractive to young people in the cities of East Asia. It gives them a sense of being modern, perhaps even of being free. At present, some of the world's greatest jazz musicians are Japanese. In the spring of 2000 the Kennedy Center in Washington, D.C., hosted a "Japanese Jazz Jam," three days of jazz concerts featuring

Japanese performers exclusively, including the all-female trio, "Groovin Girls."[18] In Japan, aging sumo wrestlers become rap stars. Equally striking is the gospel singing fad that swept Japan after the Whoopi Goldberg film *Sister Act* played there and led hundreds of Japanese to Harlem, where a workshop for Japanese gospel singers opened in 1998.[19] Thai students rallying to overthrow the dictatorship in October 1973 sang American folk songs, songs of protest. A few years ago a Thai intellectual of that generation complained wistfully that the current crop of Thai students didn't even know who Bob Dylan was.[20]

Modern dance has also been exported by the United States to East Asia. Hardly known in China before the 1980s, it was developed there with the help of the North Carolina–based American Dance Festival. Winners of a 1986 choreography competition in Beijing were granted scholarships to study at the American school, which subsequently sent teachers to an academy in Guangzhou. The Guangdong Modern Dance Company gave its first performance at home in 1990 and has performed internationally ever since. Its programs often use American music, but the works by Chinese choreographers are based on "their own tradition, culture and individual creativity."[21]

Probably the greatest American influence on popular culture in Japan, as in much of the rest of the world in the 1920s and 1930s, was the Hollywood film with its vision of the American dream. The government of the United States did press countries to open their doors to American films, as it did for other American products. The decision to see the film, however, was made by individuals, who appear to have been delighted by images of the lavish material consumption of Americans. The Japanese government in the interwar period sponsored a cultural movement stressing the differences between Japan and the West, exulting in the homogeneity of Japanese culture, but the avant-garde preferred Hollywood's message.[22] Today, in China, official efforts to limit the number of American motion pictures imported are undermined by the government's failure to prevent the circulation of pirated prints. Hollywood may be cheated out of some of its profits, but the culture it promotes is irrepressibly attractive in China.

Japanese visual arts—painting, printmaking, and photography—were also influenced by interaction with Americans, although not always in the direction of Americanization. Japanese painters were persuaded by Ernest Fenollosa, an American who emerged at the close of the nineteenth century as the foremost historian, museum curator, and occasional dealer of Japanese art, that wealthy American collectors were eager to buy *traditional* style paintings. He urged Japanese artists, with considerable success, to paint for that market rather than move on to the modern international styles that intrigued some of them. In this instance American influence was "reactionary," supporting illiberal movements in Japanese society, those most fearful of political and cultural Westernization.[23] Similarly, the interest of American collectors, such as James Michener and Oliver Statler, rekindled Japanese interest in printmaking.

Japanese photography, on the other hand, was changed by American visual arts. Not surprisingly, the Japanese were attracted initially to the work of Americans who had been influenced by Japanese aesthetics. Shinzo Fukuhara, who played a major role in the emergence of modernist photography in Japan, was influenced by the style of the American photographer Alvin Langdon Coburn, himself a student of Japanese art.[24] More recent Japanese efforts, however, depart further from tradition. Daido Moriyama, whose art was exhibited in 1999 by the Japan Society in New York, credits the influence of the work of the American photographer William Klein—and of an Andy Warhol catalogue—for his distinctive approach.[25]

Like most young artists of East Asia questing after modernity or a new aesthetic, the pre–World War II generation of Chinese painters studied Western art in nearby Tokyo or exotic Paris. After the war, nontraditional artists from Taiwan often studied or went to live in the United States, as did most members of the Fifth Moon group, a prominent band of painters led by Liu Kuo-sung. To those on the mainland, the United States was unattractive and unavailable until the 1980s. In contrast to the Soviet failure to sell Kvass, Soviet socialist realism greatly influenced Chinese art. A younger generation, however, hearing Joan Lebold Cohen's lectures on modern American art in 1979 and seeing her slides featuring the work of painters such as Jackson Pollock and Willem de Kooning, was exhilarated.[26] Although Beijing relaxed its control significantly in the 1990s, artistic freedom still does not exist in the People's Republic, and some artists have left for the United States and Europe. Some of those who remain, He Duoling, Zhu Yigong, and Yuan Min among them, have found an acceptable compromise with the authorities by painting in the style of the New England artist Andrew Wyeth, known for his own form of realism.[27]

If any part of American culture rivals the motion picture in popularity in Japan, China, Taiwan, Korea, and the Philippines, it would probably be sports, specifically basketball and baseball. At the beginning of the twentieth century, sports were considered undignified in China. Shirley Garrett tells the wonderful (probably apocryphal) story of the Shanghai gentleman who, "while watching four Americans play tennis, inquired why they didn't hire someone else to do it for them."[28] She credits the YMCA with introducing sports in China and founding modern physical education there.

When I lived in Beijing in 1986, all my television set seemed to offer was a choice between *Hunter* and the National Basketball Association. I was not surprised to learn, years later, that Michael Jordan was the world's most popular figure among young Chinese. In 1999, the Dallas Mavericks selected 7' 1" Wang Zhizhi in the NBA draft, but he was not allowed to leave his team in China. In 2000, Chinese authorities refused to allow Yao Ming, the 7' 6" star of the Shanghai Sharks, to play in an American tournament, fearing he would defect to the NBA.[29] In Tokyo, the journalist Patrick Smith came across "Hooptown Harajuku," a place where for $60 an hour six Japanese could imagine they were American inner-city athletes, playing three-on-three, on an asphalt basketball court, covered with graffiti provided by the owner, and surrounded by a chain link fence, just like in New York City.[30]

Anyone who has ever watched or read about Little League baseball championships is aware of the longtime dominance of teams from Taiwan. Taiwan's love of baseball appears to derive not from its years as an American protectorate, but as a benefit of Japanese colonialism. After World War II, the Guomindang tried to suppress baseball, but the arrival of the American military in the 1950s revived the game on the island. The Korean experience was similar: the game was introduced by the Japanese and nurtured by Americans after the war. Baseball is now second only to soccer in popularity in Korea. The Koreans have also performed well in international basketball competitions.

It is, of course, the Japanese who have made baseball *their* national pastime, while Americans have chosen to shift their affection to sports incorporating more body contact—football, hockey, and basketball. Baseball in Japan goes back to the Meiji era and has been played professionally there since 1935, but it is intercollegiate baseball that is the country's major sport. Those who are familiar with the game as it is played in Japan—or who have read Robert Whiting's books[31]—are aware that it is played differently there, so much so that expatriate American ballplayers have had great difficulty adapting. We might call it American baseball with Japanese characteristics, a group sport stressing harmony and discipline, with little room for individualism. Nonetheless, the Japanese have been exporting players to the United States in recent years, and there are several Japanese players—and an occasional Korean or Chinese player—on major-league teams.

In 1934, the great Babe Ruth played on tour in Japan. His appearances were an enormous success despite the tensions that had arisen between the governments of Japan and the United States following the Manchurian crisis. The affection that the Japanese public bestowed on Ruth led the American government to consider using him as a peace negotiator in 1945.[32] It was a wild, crazy idea that never got off the ground, but it certainly compared favorably to the alternative chosen to end the war.

Two other examples of American popular culture that have been freely and happily received by Japanese and other East Asians—to the disgust of intellectuals all over the world—are Disneyland and McDonald's. Two scholarly analyses of the Tokyo version of Disneyland, by Mary Yoko Brannen and Aviad E. Raz, reject the idea that the theme park, the most successful in the world, is evidence of American cultural imperialism. On the contrary, they both argue that Tokyo Disneyland is a form of *Japanese* cultural imperialism. Brannen explains that "the commodified cultural artifacts . . . are recontextualized in Japanese terms."[33] Raz describes the "active appropriation of Disney by the Japanese."[34]

Although the owners initially wanted to duplicate the original Disneyland, to give visitors a sense that they were on a foreign vacation, they were forced to modify their product to suit Japanese taste. Among other things, they had to abandon their plan to serve only Western food. Their visitors demanded and now are offered sushi, tempura, and curry as well. In Tokyo Disneyland, the Japanese get a sanitized, Japanized version of America, an idealized America, "showcased by and for the Japanese."[35] People from the countryside no longer see a visit to the park as a pilgrimage to America. Indeed, many Japanese children, having grown up with a Japanese-speaking Mickey Mouse, think America's favorite rodent is Japanese. This pattern of Asians in control, reshaping or imagining American cultural artifacts to be their own, is repeated endlessly throughout East Asia.

Some years ago, Ariel Dorfman and Armand Mattelart deconstructed the Disney comics, specifically Donald Duck, as an example of American cultural imperialism, an effort by Americans to brainwash readers with American capitalist ideology. Walt Disney was doubtless a very disagreeable fellow with decidedly illiberal views, but it is highly unlikely that very many of the children of East Asia who read the comics, see the cartoons, or visit the theme parks come away from them inculcated with Disney's vision of the world.

And then there is McDonald's, *Golden Arches East,* as James L. Watson titled his delightful book.[36] His most recent data indicate that the number of McDonald's in the region has doubled between 1995 and 1999. There are approximately 3,000 of them in Japan alone, 235 in China as of June 1999, and 158 in Hong Kong (one for every 42,000 residents).[37] There are probably over 1,000 more elsewhere in East Asia, everywhere except Indochina (but look for Kentucky Fried Chicken in Vietnam) and Burma—where American influence of any kind seems minimal. So great is the attraction of a "Big Mac" that Beijing students failed in their effort to organize a boycott of McDonald's and other American companies in the wake of the bombing of China's Belgrade embassy in 1999.

The evidence is clear that McDonald's is different in various parts of the region. The franchisees are eager to accommodate local preferences. The most obvious difference from a McDonald's in the United States is that Asians don't treat it as a place to grab a bite and run. It is not a fast food restaurant in that sense. Customers in Asia are much more likely to linger, to meet there to talk or to study. In most places other than Japan, where public sanitation has long been part of the culture, McDonald's is best known for its clean toilets. And these appear to be having an impact on local practices as people begin to associate clean toilets with sanitary food handling and other restaurants, hoping to remain competitive, attempt to match McDonald's practices.

Parents in East Asia view McDonald's as a safe place for their children to hang out. Women in Japan and Korea find it a comfortable place to meet without men and alcohol. And there is a growing tendency throughout the area to perceive McDonald's as local rather than American. There are many stories of Asian children traveling anxiously in the United States who were relieved at last by the sight of the Golden Arches, the realization that their "native" food was available in America. It seems clear that in Beijing, however, McDonald's is still perceived as a taste of America, as something Chinese tourists have to try, just as rural folk once lined up for Beijing duck.

In Beijing and in Hong Kong, and very likely wherever it exists in China, McDonald's has become the place of choice for children's birthday parties. As the Chinese become more affluent, as their society becomes more commercialized and their country is integrated into the global economy, eating habits are changing. Several of the essays in the anthropologist Jun Jing's recent *Feeding China's Little Emperors: Food, Children, and Social Change* stress the role of children as catalysts in the transformation of Chinese culture.[38] In his introduction, Jing notes the discomfort of older Chinese who feel rejected by children's preference for Western fast foods, a very mundane example of the pain that cultural change often causes.

The essay by Eriberto P. Lozada, Jr., on Kentucky Fried Chicken (KFC) restaurants in China is particularly instructive on the domestication of the company's operations, on how "a formerly exotic, imported food has been transformed into a familiar and even intimate type of cuisine."[39] KFC, too, has transcended the political tensions in Chinese-American relations, reopening only a week after the Tiananmen disaster in 1989. Indeed, the People's Liberation Army quartered and fed some of its troops in the Qianmen branch of the restaurant when it occupied Tiananmen Square. The most striking evidence of KFC's ability to adapt to local conditions has been the marginalization of Colonel Sanders, found to be unappealing to Chinese children. In his place, a new icon, *Qiqi* ("Chicky") appeared, a young chicken wearing an American baseball cap—although tourists still pose for pictures with the colonel's statue. Lozada attributes KFC's success in China to this adaptability, in addition to its high standards of sanitation and consistent quality.

But the best story about American fast food in China is one that James Watson relates from his research in Hong Kong. In 1995 the Hong Kong Department of Education devised an "induction program" for children arriving from the mainland to prepare them for entering the public schools. The program included visits to a sports center, a library, a shopping mall, a ride on the subway, and, finally, a stop at McDonald's for a Big Mac, fries, and a Coke at government expense. Welcome to Hong Kong.

One last example of East Asians looking to an image of the United States to chart their course can be found in the immigration policies of the new nation-states that emerged in Southeast Asia in the 1950s. What were they to do with the Chinese who flocked to their shores? With the Indians the British had left behind? Wang Gungwu tells us that "the melting pot model of the United States . . . was immensely influential."[40] Believing that assimilation had worked in the United States, Southeast Asian governments incorporated the American model into their programs.

In all of these examples, we see people freely choosing to adopt, consume, participate in, and enjoy something specifically American, or making choices influenced by their vision of the United States. All of these choices result in changes to local culture, changes in the society, "Americanization." In the absence of any form of coercion, these changes cannot reasonably be labeled cultural imperialism.

Perhaps more to the point, as Asians absorbed American cultural influences, they modified them to suit themselves, as we have seen. The impulse may have come from the United States, but the product is a hybrid, sometimes hardly recognized by Americans who encounter it, sometimes misperceived by locals as indigenous. Again, there is little to suggest that Asians who choose these hybrids feel less Chinese or

Japanese as a result—although many probably feel more cosmopolitan, more modern, at least those who are aware that they are encountering an American cultural product.

But it is clear that these societies that have adopted so many elements of American culture have redefined themselves. Chinese culture, for example, is not today what it was a generation ago—which should come as no great surprise since the Chinese have been redefining themselves for several thousand years. As Zhou Enlai once said, China has always had "an ability to absorb what is outstanding in the culture of other nations."[41] What is new is that part which was originally American, reflecting the relatively recent American dominance of East Asia. What also appears to be new is the mass appeal of foreign culture, its impact on popular culture. Culture transfer is not occurring merely as a result of efforts by elites to modernize their countries, but by popular demand among peoples whose eyes have been opened to the choices available as a result of television, film, CDs, and increased contact with foreigners.

Before turning to those cases in which the American government made a determined effort to shape the culture of Asian peoples along lines consistent with American values and tastes, I want to consider the role of American Protestant missionaries in China and Korea. They were important in Japan as well, but primarily in the late nineteenth century, when they contributed to Meiji-era efforts toward modernization. These men and women who left their homes to risk their lives among the "heathens" were not government agents, but neither was their presence always freely accepted by the people whose souls they hoped to save. Initially, they operated as part of the treaty system, the "unequal treaties" forcibly imposed upon Asian countries in the nineteenth century by the Western powers, including the United States. At least until the 1920s, outside of the Japanese empire, missionaries were the beneficiaries of "gunboat diplomacy," often protected from hostile locals by warships. And sometimes the Christianity they offered was not adopted freely, as when hungry people, "rice Christians," joined the church to avoid starvation. But if their work was not of a piece with that of the secular missionaries—the social engineers imposed on the Philippines and Japan by the American government—neither was it accepted quite as eagerly as were the elements of American culture emulated by men and women seeking modernity or the roots of American wealth and power.

As Paul A. Cohen demonstrated many years ago, the impact of the missionaries was subversive.[42] They came with the deliberate intent of changing indigenous cultures, of having the people among whom they preached abandon their traditional gods and forms of worship. In China and Korea they attacked the Confucian underpinnings of the existing social order. Of course, they encountered resistance, often violent resistance, which cost some of them their lives and required foreign military intervention to protect others. In China their converts were relatively few, yet the missionaries, perhaps especially the Americans, did contribute enormously to changing and modernizing China. In Korea, Christianity has taken root, spreading rapidly after the Second World War, largely under the leadership of native Christians. But American Protestant missionaries also had an impact on Korean culture, not least during the years when Korea was part of the Japanese empire.

In Korea the scale of the missionary effort was small relative to church activity in China, but it was predominantly American and, if judged by the percentage of Christians today, infinitely more successful. Even Kim Il Sung's mother was a Christian. By the late 1990s, 25 percent of the Korean people proclaimed themselves to be Christians. But the American missionaries' earliest impact was in furthering Korea's modernization and encouraging Korean patriotic resistance to the Japanese colonial administration. Toward the end of the nineteenth century and in the few years of the twentieth before Japan seized control of the peninsula, Americans, most notably Dr. Horace Allen,[43] contributed to the development of Western-style education and medical practices in Korea. Young progressive Korean aristocrats, associating Christianity with America, looked to the missionaries for new solutions to problems of national development—and received advice on constructing railroads, waterworks, power stations, and communication facilities, the basic infrastructure required for industrialization.[44]

In addition, the American missionaries (and the Australians and Canadians as well) attracted followers by encouraging them to resist Japanese efforts to impose Japanese culture on the Koreans, specifically by urging them to reject the demand of colonial authorities for Shinto worship.[45] Han Woo-keun has contended that "the progressive, democratic spirit of American Protestantism made the institutions founded by missionaries the natural breeding places for leaders of the resistance."[46] Missionary women joined with Korean believers in a range of activities perceived by the Japanese as provocative—and inconsistent with official American efforts to acquiesce in Japanese imperialism in Korea.[47] The missionaries tried to protect Korean patriots from persecution by the Japanese, and the Koreans in turn converted hymns learned in American Protestant churches into patriotic songs (ch'angga).[48]

In China, the Americans probably were never a majority among Protestant missionaries and constituted the largest single group for only a few years in the 1920s and 1930s. Their contribution to China's modernization, however, was striking. The centerpiece of the American effort was the Christian colleges. Jessie Lutz, the foremost student of the colleges, describes them as mediators of Western civilization, examples of Western education, and training grounds for anti-imperialist nationalists.[49] They became attractive to Chinese students after the abolition of the traditional civil service examinations in 1905, but did not enroll substantial numbers until the late 1920s, peaking in the 1940s at 15 to 20 percent of all college students in China. They were important centers for the study of science and mathematics, as well as English. They pioneered in medical and agricultural research, introduced the study of library science, and helped initiate college-level education for women. Young Chinese, disdainful of their country's traditional culture, found alternatives in the Christian colleges—without becoming Christians. And the graduates of the colleges met the state's need for teachers, educational planners, and administrators in the 1930s. Some continued in these roles after the establishment of the People's Republic and the absorption of the Christian colleges into the national university system.

Similarly, the Young Men's Christian Association (YMCA) contributed to China's modernization in important ways, attracting young urban Chinese with nonreligious teachings. Early in the Republican era, from the revolution of 1911 to the mid-1920s, it offered access to the skills they wanted and could utilize, along with the values of middle-class reformers steeped in the ethos of the Progressive movement in America. The YMCA jolted a rising Chinese middle class, especially in the coastal cities, into action to rescue their communities from corruption and disease, much as Progressive reformers were doing in the United States.[50]

Quite early in the American missionary encounter with China, medical services and education were perceived as a means of overcoming resistance to the missionary presence. The missionary doctor Peter Parker was able to play an enormously important role in facilitating American diplomatic approaches to China because of contacts with prominent Chinese whose afflictions he had successfully treated.[51] By the beginning of the twentieth century, many Chinese officials and intellectuals recognized the value of Western medicine and were receptive to efforts to train Chinese doctors and nurses. Shortly after the First World War, however, the missionary medical effort was overshadowed by a major Rockefeller Foundation effort to establish "scientific medicine" in China. It should be noted, however, that John D. Rockefeller, Jr., consistently perceived his activities in China as an extension of the missionary endeavor. The foundation funded the creation of the Peking Union Medical College (PUMC), dedicated to providing the finest medical education available.[52] It recruited an international faculty of exceptional quality and delivered the education promised. Unfortunately, PUMC's elite approach allowed for the graduation of only 313 doctors in the twenty years of its existence, most of whom situated themselves in the coastal cities. It did not begin to meet the needs of hundreds of millions of Chinese in the countryside. On the other hand, PUMC faculty and students made important contributions to medical knowledge, succeeding in attacks on several diseases endemic in China. Its graduates dominated medical school faculties and health bureaucracies not only in late Republican China, but also long after the establishment of the People's Republic—at least until the depths of the Cultural Revolution.

By the mid-1930s it was evident to some Chinese leaders and several foundation representatives that China's peasantry needed more immediate relief than PUMC's trickledown approach could provide. China was in desperate need of rural reconstruction: land reform, agricultural extension programs, and public health services. Chinese reformers, the Christian colleges, and the Rockefeller Foundation joined forces in an effort to transform the countryside. Yan Yangzhu ("Jimmy" Yen), Christian convert, Yale graduate, and sometime YMCA employee, developed the Mass Education Movement, designed to bring a minimal level of literacy to rural China.[53] Ultimately, his efforts were linked to an innovative public health program devised by Rockefeller's Dr. John Grant and designed to create a basic rural health delivery system. Agricultural programs designed to improve productivity were also incorporated into Yan's efforts. At Nanjing University, the Christian college where the most advanced agricultural research in China was being conducted, J. Lossing Buck spun off ideas on land utilization, population control, and water conservancy.[54] Regrettably, the government of Jiang Jieshi was not interested in land reform and leery of mass mobilization. It was left to the Chinese Communists to implement comparable programs, primarily after 1949. Yan won American government support for his Joint Commission on Rural Reconstruction in 1948—too late for this program to be carried out on the mainland, but it revolutionized landholding on Taiwan from 1949 to 1953.[55] Even Jiang found it expedient to support these programs when he was consolidating his hold over Taiwan, where the local landowners were his rivals rather than his supporters as on the mainland.

In retrospect, it is clear that the impact of missionaries on Chinese culture was not quite what the mission boards back in America had anticipated. China did not become a Christian country, nor were the conversion rates nearly as impressive as in Korea. The years of greatest American missionary influence, the 1920s and 1930s, were also years in which the social gospel was a powerful force in the American church. Most of the missionaries had minimal theological training and only a general knowledge of Christianity.[56] They went to China primarily as teachers and to meet China's specific needs for modernization. They were less concerned with saving souls than with improving the lives of the Chinese people—and they were remarkably successful, at least in the fields of higher education and medical research and teaching. Also important were the campaigns against foot-binding and other practices demeaning to women. The value of missionary programs is underscored by their success in Asia in the years after World War II, when the U.S. government supported many of them in developing countries all over Asia.

Today the United Board for Christian Higher Education in Asia assists over 100 Protestant colleges in the region, active even in Vietnam, Cambodia, and Burma.

Finally, there are the cases of forced Americanization, beginning at the turn of the century, in the Philippines, when President William McKinley accepted the "White Man's burden" and agreed to attempt to civilize the Filipino people. First Filipino opposition to the American occupation of the islands had to be crushed—and it was, brutally. An estimated 200,000 Filipino civilians were killed in the fighting, and at least another 500,000 died of war-related famine and disease.[57] Once the situation was brought under control, the Americans set out to remold Filipino society in America's image, to create a liberal democratic society modeled on the United States. Glenn Anthony May, a leading American student of Filipino history, calls the American occupation an "experiment in self-duplication."[58] The Americans failed. Ostensibly, they had complete control of Filipino society, free rein, for forty years, but they did not create a liberal democracy. They did not instill the Filipinos with American political culture. "People Power" and Cory Aquino have come and gone, but the wretchedness of life in the Philippines persists. The recent surge of "People Power Lite" that forced out President Joseph "Erap" Estrada brought with it little prospect for improvement. What went wrong?

First of all, there was the racist arrogance of perceiving the

Filipinos as empty vessels, waiting, even eager to be filled with American values. Obviously there was an indigenous Malay culture with an overlay of three hundred years of Spanish indoctrination, influenced as well by centuries of Chinese immigration, which was not to be brushed aside easily. The syncretism, the hybridization that actually occurred under American colonial rule was always the most likely outcome.

Second, the Americans were inexperienced colonial rulers, uncertain of their goals and unsure of their methods. Although there was considerable skepticism among them as to whether the Filipinos would ever be ready for independence, or even want it, it was essential to promise eventual independence and to take steps to prepare the people for it. The promise of independence and gestures toward it were essential to win the support of the Filipino elite, without whose cooperation it would be difficult and expensive to govern the islands. These expectations were also essential to maintain support for empire at home. Anti-imperialists in the United States could be pacified by the argument that the occupation was merely for tutelary purposes—and by evidence that the Filipinos were willing participants in the experiment in social engineering.

Beyond the promise of independence, Americans were agreed on taking steps to create democratic institutions, including elected municipal governments, a national legislature, and a civil service. But they were initially unable to conceive of the socioeconomic reforms necessary to distribute wealth and power equitably in the society. The first series of American officials were conservatives, hostile to the progressive reforms being advanced in American society and better able to block them in the Philippines. They tended to view Filipinos much as they viewed African Americans at home, as backward and childlike. They had little understanding of the needs of peasants or the poor in the barrios. Although American officials did plan for the economic development of the islands, the U.S. Congress had little interest and blocked potentially useful programs. Congressmen were much more concerned with protecting the interests of their constituents—American sugar producers, for example. And when American officials did attempt to carry out reforms, including efforts to create a nation of small landholders in accordance with the Jeffersonian vision, they were thwarted by the Filipino elite.

By all accounts, the crucial failing of the American colonial experiment in the Philippines was the decision of officials to ally with the local elite, however sensible this may have seemed in the early years of American rule. The U.S. government succeeded in preventing Americans from plundering the islands, but it could not contain the avarice of the oligarchy to which it handed the power to execute—or not execute—policy. The elite collaborators had de facto veto power over social and economic policy, and they showed little if any concern for the well-being of countrymen other than their extended family and clients. James Fallows has suggested that there is no country in Asia in which people treat each other worse.[59] The Philippines is what it is today because the United States failed in its efforts to change the political culture. In this case, American cultural imperialism proved to be a paper tiger.

Of course, this is not to suggest that Americans, in their days as colonial rulers or in their Cold War days as neocolonial exploiters, left the Filipinos without scars. Filipino cultural nationalists decry what Americans might consider their greatest contribution—public education, in *English,* giving the disparate peoples of the various islands a common language. Nationalists argue that this practice defilipinized the people, who were subjected to courses which glorified American life and American purposes in the Philippines, while erasing the history of the resistance—and of American atrocities.[60]

Stanley Karnow, in his Pulitzer Prize–winning history of the American colonial era in the Philippines, describes his initial trip to the islands. He found most of the people he met speaking Americanized English, educated in the United States or American schools, and highly knowledgeable about the United States, as if "they were some kind of lost American tribe that had somehow become detached from the U.S. mainland and floated across the Pacific."[61]

Filipino popular culture was unquestionably Americanized. The cultural life of the islands, especially Manila, but also wherever there were American military bases, was dominated by American movies, music, and dances. Filipino movies were generally mere rehashes of American films, as were soap operas and comic strips. Filipinos learned to play baseball and to worship movie stars and basketball players.[62] Educated Filipinos of the 1920s perceived culture in terms of what was created in New York and Hollywood. There is a wonderful phrase used to describe this process: "Three hundred years in a Spanish convent and forty years in Hollywood have left Filipinos culturally dispossessed," so immersed in American culture that leftist NPA (National People's Army) guerrillas wore UCLA T-shirts.[63]

What does it all add up to? Unlike the examples of peoples who chose to adopt aspects of American culture, the Filipinos had it imposed on them. But the *Ilustrados,* the indigenous elite, successfully resisted any change that threatened their wealth and power. They used even well-intentioned American reforms to bolster their own position. The peasants, and the poor generally, are probably worse off relative to the elite than they were when the Americans first arrived.

American popular culture, however, became and remains a central part of Filipino life, certainly in the urban areas. In the end, it seems clear that Americanization has been superficial, a blemish on the skin, but, like a tattoo, not easily removed. It is hardly likely that in our lifetime, the Americanization of popular culture in the Philippines will give way to something more pleasing to cultural nationalists. Return visits and cultural remittances by the rapidly increasing number of Filipinos living in the United States serve to reinforce Americanization. The American impact will be long-term, if not indeed permanent. It is equally unlikely that the oligarchs will allow a New Deal for the Filipino people. In sum, it would be difficult to conclude that the encounter with the United States did much for Filipino society or culture. The Filipinos might well have been better off with a less benign colonial master and the satisfaction of fighting for and eventually winning their independence.

But, if I read John Dower correctly, forced Americanization has had one great success: the occupation of Japan.[64]

The Americans who went to occupy Japan in 1945 were a very different people with a culture very different from those who arrived in Manila at the beginning of the century. They were no less committed to transforming the target country into a duplicate of their own, to turning Japan into a liberal democracy, but the American conception of what such a society should be and of government's role in shaping it had changed after the New Deal and the experiences of the 1930s. American culture was dynamic: it had changed, but the fundamental premise, the superiority of liberal democracy over all other forms of government known to man, persisted.

Of even greater importance was the fact that the Japanese people of 1945 were very different from the Filipinos of 1900. The Japanese were the most "modern" of Asian peoples, and they perceived, in defeat, that something was wrong with their culture. They seem to have had a sense of comparative culture that came right out of the early anthropological studies of Edward Sapir (1884–1939): that in a clash between people of different cultures, the victor had demonstrated the superiority of its culture. They were ready to be Americanized.

Of course, Americanization was not what the Japanese political elite had in mind. The demilitarization that the Americans demanded was certainly tolerable, at least in the short run. Military men had led the nation to ruin. They were discredited and had few, if any, defenders. But the civilian leadership that remained was appalled by the idea of democracy for Japan. Yoshida Shigeru, the dominant politician of the occupation era, expressed his conviction that the Japanese people were incapable of self-government.[65] Certainly his views were shared by virtually all of his leading contemporaries.

The immediate postwar Japanese cabinet resigned in October 1945, in objection to the occupation authorities' first order removing restrictions on political, civil, and religious liberty. It appears to have been freedom of the press that they found least tolerable. And Japanese leaders consistently dragged their feet and obstructed as best they could the American efforts to create a liberal democracy in Japan. Without doubt it was their intention to erase the American-dictated reforms as soon as the Americans went home—but the Japanese people got in their way: they liked democracy, and Japan was stuck with it.

Japan's ruling elite also despised American popular culture, considering it vulgar in comparison to the European culture many admired. Surely it was inferior to Japanese culture. But it did not take long for the Japanese to produce gum as well as chew it. The motion picture industry was liberated from Japanese government control, although not from U.S. government control, and became Americanized rather than merely modernized. The kissing scenes the Americans allowed may have been shocking to Japanese sensibilities, but they could easily be perceived as portraying general Western practice. Linda Erlich notes, however, that the films were teeming with American icons, such as chewing gum and jazz—and a changing image of women.[66]

Americans controlled radio broadcasts and filled them with propaganda selling American-style democracy *and* jazz and folk songs, of which Stephen Foster's work appears to have been the most popular (as I found it to be with some urban Chinese who came of age in the immediate postwar era).[67] Dower makes a point of the role of the "pan-pan girls" who catered to the GIs and became trend-setters in their imitation of American ways. He notes that this was an unusual case of the lower classes providing leadership in cultural change.[68] And, of course, there was inevitably a counter-culture among the young, imitating the GIs, soaking up what they imagined to be American culture.

As in the Philippines, the American occupation authorities concluded it was expedient to work with the indigenous elite.

Given the degree of existing political organization in Japan, the Americans chose to rule indirectly, through Japanese officials. The results, however, were very different from what they were in the Philippines. To be sure, the Americans eventually returned control of the government to the local elite, but not before they had carried out reforms and forced upon them a new constitution which together shattered old authoritarian structures and made reversal impossible.

In Japan the Americans carried out a successful land reform, strengthened the unions, opened up the educational system, advanced the rights of women, and provided for a free press. These were radical reforms, and there was enormous popular support for them among a politically mobile people who were able to retain these new rights and privileges when the Americans handed power back to the old conservative elite. Most students of the occupation credit the American-crafted constitution forced on Japan for protecting the rights the occupation gave the Japanese people. Amending it was not made easy. Grumble as they may about having been robbed of their "Japaneseness," conservatives have not been able to discard it.

In one sense, the Japanese were extraordinarily lucky. The occupation began at a time when New Deal liberalism was still a powerful current in American society and among the men and women who staffed the offices of the occupation authorities. A decade or two earlier, the socioeconomic reforms pressed on the Japanese would have been inconceivable to Americans. Three or four years later, as Americans became increasingly conservative at home, such reforms would have been dismissed as communism, or "creeping socialism" at best. And indeed, the so-called "reverse course," the turn to the right in occupation policies that began around 1948, reflected these changes in American society at least as much as they were a product of the emerging Cold War.

One might argue that the Japanese people were also fortunate that the U.S. Department of State's experts on Japan, enamored of traditional Japanese culture and closely tied to the conservative Japanese elite, were initially denied a significant role in occupation policy. The department's most prominent Japan specialist, former ambassador to Japan Joseph Grew, and his principal aide, Eugene Dooman, fought a rear-guard action against China specialists and liberal universalists eager to destroy Japan's traditional polity. Grew did not believe that Japan could ever become a democracy. Certainly the "Japan Crowd" was less inclined to impose American culture on Japan, and when this faction regained influence in the late 1940s, it did what it could to support the resistance of Japanese conservatives.[69]

In the end, as Dower has argued, "Postwar Japan was a vastly freer and more egalitarian nation than imperial Japan had been."[70] Even when most of the Americans went home and conservatives regained control, there was more room in Japan for the political left than there was in the United States at the time. Older workers still credit Americanization for their relatively enhanced status; they are persuaded that the Americans helped the poor.

In terms of popular culture, those who love traditional Japanese art, music, and theater cannot help feeling that the Japanese who matured during and after the occupation have lost something. In the 1950s the most admired entertainer in Japan was Elvis Presley, followed by whichever other performers Armed Forces Radio included in the American top 40. In the 1960s the car of choice for Japanese gangsters, the *yakuzas,* was a Cadillac convertible. In the 1970s it was a Lincoln Continental. Japanese affection for Hollywood movies, ice cream, Disneyland, and McDonald's saddens some observers of Japan, but we must remember what the Japanese have gained as part of their Americanization: the right to think critically, to read whatever they want, to choose whatever mix of cultures they please.[71] Obviously, they think the price is right.

More recently, we have observed the evolution of democracy on Taiwan and in South Korea. American efforts to coerce the Guomindang to convert from a Leninist party to a democratic one failed utterly, as did American pressures on Syngman Rhee, Park Chung Hee, and Chun Doo Hwan to rein in the Korean CIA and the army and to provide a democratic alternative to the totalitarian state north of the thirty-eighth parallel.

But faced with abandonment by the United States in the 1980s, Taiwan's ruler, Jiang Jingguo, who succeeded his father, Jiang Jieshi, as president of the Republic of China, perceived the move toward democracy as the last best hope of salvaging the island's freedom—and he had scores of American-trained intellectuals to show him the way. Lee Teng-hui, Taiwan's first democratically elected president, loved to boast that he had more American Ph.D.s in his cabinet than did any American president. The beacon on the hill, extolled long ago by John Quincy Adams as an alternative to expansionism and the only appropriate way to serve America's mission to spread democracy, finally worked in Chinese society. One might argue that it was not lost on the young Chinese in Tiananmen Square in 1989.

Democracy came to Korea largely because the Korean people could no longer tolerate the corruption and brutality of their military leaders. The latter, under pressure from the United States, chose to risk an election in 1987 rather than use force against a mass uprising, as they had earlier at Kwangju. This time they—and the Korean people—were aware of American support for democratic revolution in the Philippines, and the American ambassador left no doubt as to where the United States stood. Despite the continuing anti-Americanism of many Korean demonstrators, the United States contributed mightily to their success, and the government they have enjoyed at the conclusion of the twentieth century and the outset of the twenty-first promises to become the liberal democracy the United States long hoped to see there.

One additional area worthy of consideration is political economy, the economic culture of East Asia. The American engineer W. Edwards Deming is usually credited with pointing the Japanese toward industrial quality control in 1950. Throughout the post–World War II era, the United States has kept its markets open, enabling the export-driven economies of much of East Asia to flourish—certainly those of Japan, Korea, Taiwan, and China. Wisely or not, the United States has also pressed East Asian states to move toward market economies, to open their doors to foreign goods and investments. It brought China into the global economy, as Deng Xiaoping recognized the failure of Mao Zedong's approach; it forced the economic liberalization of South Korea that Meredith Woo-Cumings credits with shifting power from the state to society; and certainly Japanese economic culture has changed, however slowly, under American pressure.[72]

As we look from our vantage point at the beginning of the twenty-first century, it is evident that much of East Asia, its political, economic, and popular culture, has been affected by the rise of American power and presence in the region. Globalization has a distinctly American flavor. Certainly for China, Japan, Korea, and Taiwan, as well as the Philippines, the United States is the center of the world.

There are several points about the process I have described that should be emphasized. First, direct coercion has had minimal success. Even in the Japanese case, after 1952 when the occupation ended there was room for the rejection of changes imposed by the occupation authorities, had that been the will of the Japanese people. Second, a better case can be made for a less direct form of coercion. Dependence on the United States for their security had an impact on the political culture of both Korea and Taiwan. Similarly, dependence on American markets was doubtless responsible for much of the trade liberalization that occurred in East Asia.

My third and final point is that enduring changes come as a matter of choice, of decision. None of the countries of East Asia was a doormat. Their people were not passive, helpless victims of American cultural imperialism. The peoples of these countries or their leaders resisted change, especially demands for democratic reforms or freer markets, manipulated Americans as best they could, and selected those parts of American culture they believed would improve the quality of their lives. They chose as we once did from old Chinatown menus: one from column A, two from column B—and with frequent modification of the recipes. They changed the ingredients to suit their own taste, creating hybrids only as American as the chop suey and chow mein once found in American restaurants were Chinese. To put it in the jargon of the specialists, to sustain a cultural transfer, there must be a core of congruence between transmitter and receiver. Americanization, to the extent that it has occurred, happened because the peoples of East Asia wanted it, and more often than not it took root in the *form* in which they wanted it.

And if this is indeed cultural imperialism, be assured that the Asians have been more successful as cultural imperialists in America than Americans have been in East Asia.

3

THE ASIANIZATION
OF AMERICA

Thomas Jefferson was probably the last American political thinker to look to Confucius for guidance.[1] I have no knowledge of any twentieth-century American leader looking to East Asia for political models—although it is clear that Henry Kissinger and Richard Nixon liked the way Mao Zedong and Zhou Enlai did business. They were probably not the only recent American leaders who would have enjoyed a state-controlled press. Unquestionably, the overwhelming majority of Americans are quite satisfied with their existing political system, and more than a few are determined to export it to the rest of the world. None of the theories emanating from East Asia in the last century, such as Mao Zedong's "democratic centralism" or Sukarno's "guided democracy," have demonstrated much appeal in the United States. In the realm of political organization, cultural transfer has been one-way, from America to Asia.

American economic culture, on the other hand, *has* been affected by East Asia in the twentieth century. During the Great Depression, Secretary of Agriculture Henry A. Wallace devised a plan to alleviate the misery of American farmers, the Agricultural Adjustment Act of 1938, based on his conception of China's Han dynasty "Ever Normal Granary."[2] More recently, many American industries have attempted to learn from Japanese management systems. The U.S. automobile industry in particular was almost overwhelmed by Japanese imports before the "Big Three" condescended to investigate the sources of Japanese success. Ezra Vogel, imagining a future Japan as number one, had aroused concerns as early as 1979.[3] Then in the late 1980s a host of analysts, including James Fallows, Chalmers Johnson, Clyde Prestowitz, and Karel van Wolferen—dubbed the "Gang of Four" by the Japanese—warned Americans that they were in an economic war, that they had to change their ways to be able to compete with Japanese-style capitalism.[4] In 1991, an anxious Congress gave the Department of Defense ten million dollars to establish a program to improve American industrial competitiveness by having engineers and managers study Japanese so they could learn about Japanese practices directly from experience in Japan.[5]

The closest we can come to any evidence of Asian efforts to *force* change on American culture would be the Japanese efforts to push the United States toward reforms that would solve its balance of payments problems without protectionist measures against Japanese exports. Early-twentieth-century American fears of the "Yellow Peril" proved groundless. The gravest concern of recent memory has been a fear that the Japanese were buying all of America's cultural icons, starting with Columbia Pictures, the Pebble Beach Golf Club, Brooks Brothers, and New York's Rockefeller Center.

There can be no doubt that cultural transfer across the Pacific has been asymmetrical. Historians, political scientists, and economists looking at American–East Asian relations tend to focus primarily on the realm of political economy and are struck by the efforts of Asians to learn from the United States and the West generally. They note that Americans and Europeans seem less interested in learning from Asia. Focusing on China, Paul Cohen has explained this phenomenon in terms of power relationships in the nineteenth and twentieth centuries and the sense of superiority felt by Westerners.[6] But the implication that the ideas of the people of East Asia have not interested Americans, have not influenced American life, requires closer examination.

It is clear that the interaction between East Asia and the United States has had an enormous impact on American culture. Indeed, American culture has been affected *more* profoundly than has Asian culture. The effects are intensifying, and—more so than the Americanization of East Asia—they are certain to be permanent.

In the spring 1988 issue of the *Journal of American Culture*, in an article entitled "America as a Culture," the author declared: "To be American, in sum, is to be Western."[7] Conceivably, that was once arguable. At the beginning of the twenty-first century, it is nonsense. Americans have not hesitated to turn to Asia for solutions to problems they confront with their economy, their health, their faith—or their sexual relations. Americans have been willing recipients of Asian influence on their lives and have benefited greatly from it. Asia has influenced both American popular culture and high culture: art, film, food, industry, religion, and sex. Increased contact with Asia has begun to change American values and the ways in which Americans think.

These changes in American culture pale in significance, however, when compared with the change in American identity resulting from the flow of Asians who have come as immigrants, refugees, exiles, and adoptees to live in the United States and become Americans. Among us, a *part* of us, are more than ten million people born in Asia or the descendants of people born in Asia. Current estimates indicate that they will constitute 10 percent of the population of the United States by 2050. By mid-century, 10 percent of us will be Americans whose heritage lies across the Pacific, not in Western or African civilization.

And yet these changes are still not reflected adequately in American history textbooks. For example, William H. Chafe, recently president of the Organization of American Historians, has written a superb text, *The Unfinished Journey: America Since World War II*,[8] in which he rightly emphasizes the importance of race in American society—but focuses exclusively on African Americans, ignoring the role of Asian Americans and the impact of the postwar immigration from Asia.

The United States in the year 2000 had a governor, two senators, several congressmen and women, a cabinet member (a second appointed in 2001), and countless federal and state officials of East Asian ancestry, some of Asian birth. Asian Americans are becoming increasingly active politically and are beginning to influence the foreign policy of the United States. They have yet to achieve the influence of the Jews, the Irish, or the Cubans, but it is only a matter of time. Now, when increasing numbers of Americans eat Asian food, attend Asian movies, practice Asian martial arts, and look to Buddhism for spiritual guidance, when American geopolitical strategists focus increasingly on Pacific affairs, when more and more American citizens are ethnically Asian, it is time to recognize the "Asianization" of America.

The impact of East Asia on American popular culture is the easiest place to begin. Asian influence on film in the United States began with motion pictures produced in Asia that penetrated the foreign film market, most commonly art film houses and film festivals, and continued with Hollywood-produced copy-cat films. My generation, attending college in the early 1950s, came of age with Ingmar Bergman. In the years since then, Japanese and Chinese filmmakers have been tremendously successful in the United States. Akira Kurosawa is undoubtedly the most familiar of these. His *Rashomon* won an Academy Award and has become part of our vocabulary—the "Rashomon effect" is used as a metaphor for disparate views of the same incident. His *Seven Samurai* was imitated by Sam Peckinpah in *The Wild Bunch* and more obviously in John Sturges's *Magnificent Seven.* Most of Kurosawa's later films were financed by Americans, including Francis Coppola and Steven Spielberg. And of course, Japan gave us the Godzilla movies and the Mighty Morphin Power Rangers that are forever repeated on American television.

On another level, there were the wonderful Hong Kong martial arts classics that led to the cult of Bruce Lee and the Americanized spin-offs—David Carradine's *Kung Fu* television series, the various roles of Chuck Norris, a one-time student of Bruce Lee, and countless others. Hong Kong has moved to America: John Woo is now directing in the United States; Jackie Chan, Chow Yun-fat (who played opposite Jodie Foster in *Anna and the King of Siam*) and Jet Li are now Hollywood stars—while Hollywood goes to Hong Kong to make films, in the hope of penetrating the Chinese market. A. O. Scott, reviewing the film industry for the year 2000, pointed to the "near-ubiquity of Hong Kong–style action choreography" in American movies as evidence of Asian ascendance in the medium.[9]

In recent years we have had a slew of superb films by mainland Chinese directors, of whom Zhang Yimou has probably had the most impact with movies such as *Red Sorghum, Ju Dou,* and *Raise the Red Lantern,* starring the extraordinary Gong Li. And from across the strait, from Taiwan, American filmgoers have been blessed with Ang Lee and his superb *Wedding Banquet* and *Eat, Drink, Man, Woman.* His *Crouching Tiger, Hidden Dragon* flopped in China, but won four Academy Awards in the United States and earned more than $100 million at the box office. New Taiwanese Cinema's Edward Yang directed *Yi Yi,* one of the most highly praised films of 2000. Films from all three Asian venues have been very successful since the mid-1980s, and are increasingly produced in the United States. Indeed, one critic called the 2000 New York Film Festival "a celebration of Asian film."[10]

The year 2000 was notable for what might be called fusion films, American movies strongly influenced by Asia. *Ghost Dog: The Way of the Samurai* was directed by Jim Jarmusch, one of the pioneers of the American independent film movement. He calls it a "gangster samurai hip-hop eastern western." It is the story of a Mafia hit man who lives by the precepts of an eighteenth-century Japanese warrior code, the *hagakure.* He is played by Forest Whitaker, an African American actor with a long interest in Asian philosophy. One critic has focused on the sound track, created by the hip-hop master "the RZA, of the Wu-Tang Clan," whose specialty is a synthesis of African American and Asian motifs.[11]

Romeo Must Die makes no pretense to artiness. It is a standard big studio (Warner Brothers) production starring Jet Li, a martial arts master, whose earlier work in Hong Kong inspired the Oscar-winning American movie *The Matrix.* The *New York Times* reviewer referred to *Romeo*'s "relatively chaste marriage of hip-hop and kung fu" and grudgingly declared that it was bound to be a hit because of its "wall-to-wall hip-hop sound track."[12] (When theorists of cultural transfer or globalization write of hybridization, I suspect this is what they have in mind.) And for their summer entertainment, Americans delighted in the "giddily, effervescently funny" *Shanghai Noon,* described in the *New York Times* as a "slapstick kung fu horse opera."[13]

Hollywood films with Asian motifs have been criticized for a long time by Asian Americans contemptuous of the Charlie Chan films which were so popular in the 1930s and of all the others in which Caucasians were cast as Chinese or Japanese characters. A more recent complaint comes from Asian American feminists. Writing for *Ms.* magazine, Jessica Hagedorn, a Filipina American, argued that Hollywood movies trivialize or exoticize Asian women and summed up her argument neatly by declaring that "Asian women are the ultimate wet dream in most Hollywood movies."[14]

Jennifer Tung writes of watching a rerun of the 1967 James Bond film, *You Only Live Twice,* in which 007 is in bed with a Chinese woman. She asks him if he thinks Chinese girls are better and he replies, "Not better, just different—the way Peking duck is different from Russian caviar." "Dah-ling," says the Chinese woman, "I give you very best duck." Today the roles for Asian women are increasing on television and in film—and the characters tend to be more complex than the traditional sex nymph or dragon lady. Lucie Liu, nominated for an Emmy for best supporting actress on *Ally McBeal,* and who stars as a kick-boxing cop in the 2000 film version of *Charlie's Angels,* certainly does not lack sexual appeal, but the emphasis has shifted to her wit and her courage.[15] Ming-Na, who plays Dr. Jing-mei Chen on *E.R.,* is occasionally aggressive, frequently irritating, occasionally vulnerable, but never a sex object.

Tired of searching in vain for appropriate roles, Filipino Americans perform in their own Ma-Yi Theater Company founded in the Philippines in 1989 as part of the street protest against the Marcos regime. Several of the founders ended up in New York, where the company now stages off-Broadway plays written and performed by Filipino Americans. They dedicated the 2000–2001 season to the work of Han Ong, the first Filipino American to win a MacArthur "genius" grant. Several members of the group performed in the Joseph Papp Public Theater's production of Jessica Hagedorn's *Dogeaters* in 2001.[16]

Having discounted the ideological impact of Donald Duck and other Disney characters on Asian children, I am inclined to be equally dismissive of the impact of Japanese comic characters on the thinking of American readers and television viewers. Violent as many of these comic books *(manga)* and animated cartoons *(anime)* are, I do not hold them responsible for the increased violence or lack of civility in American society. "Astroboy" came to America in 1963. "Sailor Moon" came in 1995, but never caught on in the United States. More recent imports are "Pikachu" and "Pokemon." Many American video shops have a special section set aside for Japanese animated cartoons. Some children may be no more aware that these characters are Japanese than Japanese children are that Mickey Mouse is American, but surely they are as much evidence of Japanese "cultural imperialism" as Disney characters are of American.

Turning to the topic of food, I would ask a similar question: if the presence of McDonald's, Kentucky Fried Chicken, and Coca-Cola across East Asia is evidence of American cultural imperialism, what do we make of the fact that there are scores of East Asian restaurants in the United States for every McDonald's or KFC in East Asia? Chinese restaurants of every variety—there were an estimated 35,000 in the United States in 1993—continue to proliferate across the country. Americans have gone from ordering chop suey to consuming dishes fit for the most discriminating Chinese gourmet— dishes from every province known for its cuisine, and perhaps a few that are not. There are even kosher Chinese restaurants like Genghis Cohen in Los Angeles and the late Moshe Dragon in Rockville, Maryland.[17] Muslim dietary requirements were met by a *halal* Chinese restaurant in northern New Jersey that opened in 2000 to meet the needs of the growing Muslim community there.

Raw fish, which Americans once perceived as bait for catching larger fish, is now ingested by the ton every day in the major cities of the United States. There is a glatt kosher sushi restaurant in New York City. Thai restaurants have caught on, as have Korean, Vietnamese, Indonesian, and, more sparingly, Burmese, Malaysian, Filipino, and Cambodian. And Asian grocery stores, no longer confined to "ghettos" such as Chinatown, Japantown, Manilatown, or Little Saigon, seem to pop up everywhere. Standard supermarkets in "white-bread" communities now offer fresh sushi and springrolls every day, in addition to stocking their shelves with a wide range of Asian vegetables, canned goods, and instant noodles. There are also scores of cookbooks available to facilitate preparing those exotic foods at home. And with all these wonderful foods, Americans drink Tsingtao, Sapporo, Kirin, Asahi, and Singha beer—perhaps not as much as Asians drink Coke and Pepsi, but considerably more than Asians drink American beer.

Donna Gabaccia, in her *We Are What We Eat: Ethnic Food and the Making of Americans,* argues that eating is how Americans overcome their cultural conservatism.[18] They are cautious about people who are ethnically different, but curious enough to approach them by eating their food (Freud undoubtedly would have had fun with this explanation). Gabaccia also points to the "fusion" restaurants that began to pop up in the 1980s, such as Alice Waters's Chez Panisse and Wolfgang Puck's Chinois in California, Asian Nora's and the late Xing Kuba in Washington, D.C., and Blue Ginger in Wellesley, Massachusetts. For those who want the ultimate in hybridization, there is always Benihana of Tokyo, which offers mid-American cuisine served by chefs trained to have the air of samurai warriors, while promising, in the words of the founder, "no icky, sticky, slimy stuff."[19] Benihana probably laid the foundation for the incredible success of the Japanese program *Iron Chef,* now shown nationally on American television's Food Network, a contest between "culinary samurai" ("Pokemon for grown-ups") in which competing chefs demonstrate their skill with cleavers and attempt to outcook each other.[20] But of course the ultimate Japanese revenge for Commodore Perry's Black Ships was the development in 1908 and subsequent export of *ajinomoto,*[21] also known as "Accent" and just plain MSG—which has brought misery to millions of Americans.

One indication of the secure place Asian food has in the American diet came during the 1996 meeting in Seattle of the American Institute of Wine and Food. Conscious of the salience of the issue, the Institute's international conference planners chose the influence of Asian cuisine as the theme for the year and included a panel devoted to the selection of the proper wines to drink with Asian food. In brief, chili peppers were considered the greatest challenge, and the conferees agreed to recommend a German Riesling.[22] This knotty problem was confronted subsequently by Fareed Zakaria, then managing editor of *Foreign Affairs,* moonlighting as the

wine columnist for *Slate*. He recommended white wines exclusively: German wines for Chinese food, traditional dry
French wines for Japanese and Vietnamese, and Gewurtz-
traminer or Pinot Blanc for Thai and Indian.[23]

The realm of popular culture includes the martial arts
craze popularized by Bruce Lee, Chuck Norris, Steve Seager,
Jet Li, and others in hundreds of mostly bad movies. The first
judo school in America was opened by a Japanese in Seattle
early in the twentieth century.[24] T'ai chi arrived in the 1930s,
introduced by a Chinese master. Karate in America is a
post–World War II phenomenon started in Arizona by a vet-
eran who had picked it up in the Solomon Islands and continued his studies in Singapore. Tae Kwon Do was introduced
in Texas in the 1950s by a Korean student. There are scores of
variations, including the most recent craze for Muay Thai (a
particularly vicious form of kickboxing),[25] that have attracted millions of Americans of all ages. Within a ten-mile
radius of my home in a Maryland suburb of Washington,
there are at least thirteen different martial arts schools.[26]

The appeal of Asian martial arts for Americans is a bit of a
puzzle. Some of it is delight in exotica, perhaps similar to eating ethnic food—a way to approach another culture with
minimal direct contact. Most of the martial arts are also satisfying forms of exercise at a time when Americans are extraordinarily concerned about health and fitness. Because they
are forms of self-defense that do not depend on brute
strength, they are attractive to normal-size people, who can

identify with diminutive practitioners like Bruce Lee and Jet Li—if not with Steve Seagal—and fantasize about using their skill to ward off larger attackers. And some of them require a discipline that makes them especially appealing to parents.

For those less athletically inclined, there is always mah-jong. I grew up listening to the clacking of mah-jong tiles and assumed the game had been invented by Jewish ladies in New York. But, of course, it was brought over from China and attracted the attention of upper-class Americans, for whom it became a fad in the 1920s—and from whom it trickled down to the working classes when they achieved a modicum of leisure during and after World War II.

Two other aspects of American culture that have been changed by contact with East Asia cannot be categorized easily as either popular or high culture: sex and medicine. What Americans have learned from Asia about sexual practices has been examined carefully in the pages of the *Journal of American Culture.* There I learned from Stephen Gould that Asian practices having to do with preserving and enhancing one's vital energy, and using sexuality to induce altered states of consciousness, are popular in the United States; that there are Taoist sex practices that preserve *qi;* that there are scores of books, videos, and magazines on this subject aimed at New Age audiences; that there is a practice called "seminal kung fu" that prolongs the pleasure of orgasm, providing whole-body orgasms.[27]

Probably more familiar to most Americans is the surge of

interest in Chinese traditional medicine, especially acupuncture and herbal remedies and, more recently, *Qi Gong.* Herbal remedies have been known in the United States for centuries, brought over from Europe in the eighteenth century and by Asian immigrants in the nineteenth. Today the U.S. government spends approximately $50 million annually to support research in traditional Chinese medicine. The library of the National Institute of Health contains more than two thousand ancient books on Chinese herbal remedies. American companies now collect nearly half of the $20 billion spent around the world each year for these ostensibly Chinese medicines.[28]

The American Association of Acupuncture and Oriental Medicine was founded in 1981. There are probably more than two thousand member practitioners today. Acupuncture is taught now in some American medical schools and practiced by thousands of licensed non-physicians. Among the many Americans who have been helped by one or another of these practitioners are members of the Los Angeles Lakers NBA championship team. The Lakers' great star, Shaq O'Neal, is treated regularly by Shen Hsu, director of Harmony Center Acupuncture, and claims he would be unable to play without Hsu's cupping and scraping.[29]

My focus in the past has been on "high" culture,[30] but I am increasingly delighted by the weight of evidence of East Asia's influence on popular culture—and there is much more that might be examined, for example, the *karaoke* bar, or the

Tokyo Street Style vogue that has hit lower Manhattan, complete with the Tokyo Street 2000 celebration in Chelsea, with its effort to mimic Harajuku.[31] Vivienne Tam's *China Chic* discusses Chinese cultural influences, such as the collecting of Ming-style furniture and the affectation of Mao jackets.[32]

A student of socio-linguistics might enjoy the way in which elements of Japanese culture have come to be used as similes, as in a report on parents in Pelham, New York, seeking ways to pick their children's teachers without appearing to do so, a process described as a game "as stylized as a Japanese tea ceremony." A mother involved in this game described it as "a mysterious process, like Kabuki theater."[33] These are examples of Americans thinking and acting like Japanese, becoming adept at *haragei,* indirect methods of manipulating outcomes. And references to the Chinese concept of *feng shui* are becoming more frequent. Rowenta irons, for example, are sold with a brochure entitled "The Feng Shui of Ironing," which explains that a wrinkle is actually tension in the fabric, the removal of which improves the flow of *qi.*[34] In April 2000, Alex Stark, described as a *feng shui* expert, helped realign the Web site of Corcoran.com, enabling the owners to achieve a harmonious balance in cyberspace.[35] And would-be NBA stars having trouble finding the hoop can now read *The Tao of the Jump Shot.*[36] Expressions derived from East Asian languages are nearly as prevalent as those from Yiddish in contemporary American English. This Asian-influenced change

in language usage reflects changes in habits and values resulting from increased contact and greater familiarity with Asia.

Turning to high culture, to the influence of East Asia on art in
America, we might begin with the acceptance of the idea that
what Asians consider art is in fact art—a broadening of
the American aesthetic. This is tied to the story of collectors, turn-of-the-century figures like Edward Morse, Ernest
Fenollosa, and Sturgis Bigelow, all connected to the Boston
Museum of Fine Arts, as well as Charles Freer, whose collection is now part of the Smithsonian—a story I have told elsewhere.[37] More recently, a striking phenomenon is the rapid
increase in art galleries showing modern Asian and Asian
American art. New York has had an annual Asian Art Fair
since 1995.

Also of interest is Asian influence on American painters,
where two patterns are apparent. One is that of the artist who
views Asian art in a museum or catalogue and incorporates
visual ideas thus discovered into his or her own painting—
calligraphy, for example, or empty space. Robert Motherwell
painted his "Emperor of China" in 1947 from a photograph
of a portrait of a Song emperor. Franz Kline's calligraphic
work and Brice Marden's "Cold Mountain, Zen Studies"
series also fit this description. Generally these are artists
looking for a new aesthetic who find something inspiring
in Chinese or Japanese art. Alden Dow, one of the central

figures in the teaching of art in America, stumbled upon a book of Hokusai prints that opened his mind to new possibilities; he went on to develop theories of composition based on the Asian art collection at the Boston Museum of Fine Arts. His text was used for many years in the United States, and his ideas continued to be spread long afterward by his students.[38] In subsequent years, countless Americans have taken classes on Chinese or Japanese brush painting and calligraphy.

A second category of artists consists of those whose search for a new vision took them to Japan or China, where they immersed themselves in the culture, studying not only brush painting and calligraphy but religion and philosophy as well. Some spent time living in Buddhist monasteries and even became Buddhists. Two notable artists among this group are the great Northwest painters Mark Tobey and Morris Graves. The literature on Tobey stresses his longing for spirituality. In general, explanations by artists of their work are difficult to take literally, but in 1934 Tobey did go to China briefly to study Buddhism and Chinese painting, and he lived for several months in a Zen monastery near Kyoto. It is evident that Chinese and Japanese calligraphy affected his work. He once credited a rubbing he bought in Shanghai with turning him to abstract painting, to painting in black and white using a calligraphic technique he called "white writing."[39]

Graves is more obviously mystical in his paintings and prints, some of which reflect Tobey's influence. In 1927, at the age of seventeen, he shipped out on a merchantman to

East Asia and was captivated by what he saw in Japan. He returned twice in 1930 and became convinced that the Japanese did everything the right way: they accepted nature rather than resisting it. He never seems to have grappled with the contradiction between the mystical, sensitive Japan he loved and the aggressive, brutal Japanese behavior of the 1930s and 1940s. In 1935 he began to attend a Buddhist temple in Seattle and started the study of Zen, encouraged by Tobey and later by the composer John Cage. His goal, in which he was strikingly successful, was to reconcile Asian and Western aesthetics. He wanted to combine the vision of Paul Klee with the Japanese whimsical penetration of nature. He wrote wistfully of his regret that the West had not been as open to Japanese culture—presumably as a means of transcending mechanization and materialism—as Japan had been to Westernization.[40]

Graves won a Guggenheim grant to study in Japan in 1946, but the occupation authorities denied him permission to enter the country, possibly because he had been a conscientious objector during the war. It was 1954 before he succeeded in returning for five weeks. Once there, he bought Japanese art supplies, studied *kakemono*-style paper mounting, fell in love with Noh theater, and began painting in the Japanese style: brush painting with sumi ink on Japanese rice paper. He perceived himself to be adding Western commentary to traditional Japanese art. His still-life paintings continue to exhibit a flatness derived from traditional Japanese works. Ray Kass's catalogue of paintings from the Phillips Collection in Washington, D.C., contains a picture of Graves in his leek garden, circa 1973, dressed in Japanese garments, that could easily pass for a late-nineteenth-century picture of Sturgis Bigelow or any other member of Fenollosa's entourage.[41] Like them, Graves seemed to be plunging into East Asian–tinged mysticism as an escape from modernity. There can be no doubt that his psychological identity was affected profoundly by his contact with Japan.

Japanese ceramics have also fascinated Americans, at least since Edward Morse brought his collection to the Museum of Fine Arts in Boston. In the twentieth century, many American potters developed their craft in Japan.[42] *Raku* stoneware, a low-fired pottery developed in the sixteenth century by Raku Chojiro of Kyoto for the tea ceremony, has been popular with American artists since the end of World War II. Stephen Merritt, a New York potter who apprenticed with two Japanese masters, is considered by contemporary Japanese critics to be one of the world's greatest creators of Japanese ceramic art.[43]

In striking contrast to the work of Americans who find their inspiration in Asia is the work of a number of Asian-born artists who find in Western techniques a means to escape what they consider the dead hand of tradition. Early in 2000, the Guggenheim Museum in New York featured the work of the Korean-born video artist Nam June Paik. Trained as a classical musician, he seems to have been led astray by

John Cage. He became involved in the avant-garde Fluxus movement, which included Yoko Ono. One of his works, "Zen for Head," involved dipping his hair and tie into a mixture of ink and tomato juice and dragging both over a long scroll. He went on to make sculptures out of television sets and then, with the cellist Charlotte Moorman, produced some exceptionally bizarre performance art in the late 1960s, the most famous of which is Paik's "TV Bra for Living Sculpture," in which Moorman played the cello with two small functioning television sets wired to her cello and taped to her breasts. The exhibition at the Guggenheim also included a piece called "Video Buddha," another Asian motif presented in an extremely nontraditional way.[44]

The work of Brooklyn-based Xu Bing, winner of a 1999 MacArthur "genius" award, may not be quite as provocative as Paik's but it did not please Chinese authorities, who left him little choice but to emigrate to the United States. His most famous piece, "Book from the Sky," originally exhibited in Beijing just before the Tiananmen massacre, consisted of eighty-foot-long scrolls hung from the gallery ceiling; the walls of the gallery were covered with Chinese newspapers, and the floor was filled with hand-bound Chinese books. He calls his recent work "New English Calligraphy," English words that appear to be Chinese characters. He shows his work primarily in New York and other American cities but also exhibits internationally.[45]

One artist deserves mention because his experience is

quite different from that of the others I have discussed: the great sculptor Sam Gilmour, better known to most of us as Isamu Noguchi. His father was a prominent Japanese poet who, while passing through the United States, had an affair with an American woman, Leonie Gilmour, which resulted in the birth of Isamu in 1904. Papa Noguchi had already left for Japan, where he soon married a Japanese woman. Unwilling to reprise the role of Madame Butterfly, Gilmour took the boy to Japan when he was two, but Papa Noguchi had become a rabid chauvinist and appears to have been troubled by the appearance of his half-American son. When the boy was thirteen, his mother sent him back to the United States alone. Renamed Sam Gilmour, he attended high school in Indiana. It was apparent that he was not central to the life of either his father or his mother.[46]

Isamu Noguchi was a classic case of a man caught between two cultures, never secure in either. When he applied for a Guggenheim grant in 1926, he wrote of his desire to interpret East Asia for Westerners through sculpture. In 1930, he went to China for eight months and was briefly involved with a woman in the entourage of the "Young Marshal," Zhang Xueliang, the warlord who controlled Manchuria. In Beijing, Noguchi was fascinated by the Temple of Heaven, and became a student of the whimsical Chinese painter Qi Baishi. Late in the year he went to Japan and, clearly uncomfortable there, hated the country. Japanese aesthetics did not become central to his work until his return to Japan in 1950, but he did spend some months on his earlier trip wandering in search of traditional Japan. In Kyoto, he was taken in hand by Harvard's Langdon Warner and introduced to the ancient Japanese clay sculptures called *haniwa* and Zen gardens, both of which excited him. But in September 1931, appalled by Japan's aggression in Manchuria, he returned immediately to the United States.

Noguchi experienced racist attacks on his work in New York and was subsequently reminded of his strange status by the Japanese attack on Pearl Harbor. When the "relocation" camps were set up, he voluntarily interned himself. After the war he designed sets for ballet and spent time with John Cage, whose circle included many artists looking to Asia, especially to Zen Buddhism, to give new meaning to their work.

Noguchi returned to East Asia in 1949 and was entranced by Borobudur, the Buddhist Great Stupa in Java, and the Khmer sculpture at the Angkor Wat temple complex in Cambodia. In 1950, he went back to Japan. To his surprise, Japanese artists, who were eager to connect with the outside world after years of being constrained by first their own government and then the occupation authorities, greeted him as a famous *American* artist. He immersed himself in Japanese culture, and it became the dominant influence on him and his work for the rest of his life. He lived most of his remaining years in Japan, but a sculpture he designed for the Hiroshima Peace Center and park was rejected because he was an

American. In Japan, his work was always considered too Western. In the United States, it was often perceived as being too "Oriental." On the bridge between two cultures, Noguchi was forever seeking a synthesis, both in his work and in his life.

Obviously, many other American artists and architects were influenced by East Asia, or the East Asia they imagined. James McNeill Whistler was intrigued by Japanese prints and Chinese ceramics, finding new ideas in their composition and forms. John La Farge was fascinated by both Chinese and Japanese painting. Frank Lloyd Wright's architecture was influenced significantly by Japan. He saw Japanese crafts as an alternative to the machine-made products of the West. He collected and became a dealer of Japanese prints, supplementing his income from designing buildings and furniture. Helen Frankenthaler still goes to Japan to have the blocks carved for her prints. Clay Lancaster, in his book *The Japanese Influence in America,* stressed the impact of Japan on the decorative arts.[47]

American poets were also influenced by the philosophy and religion of East Asia, as well as by its poetry. Ezra Pound was probably the greatest of those who looked to East Asia, before he found Mussolini. In the 1950s, every aspiring poet tried his or her hand at *haiku.* The "Beat" poets of the 1950s and 1960s found inspiration across the Pacific, especially Gary Snyder, who studied for more than ten years at Daitokuji, a magnificent temple complex in Kyoto. Snyder won a Pulitzer Prize for his poetry in 1975 and the Bollinger Prize in 1997. And, of course, there was the notorious Allen Ginsberg, who in the 1970s made Buddhism the center of his life and thereafter taught Buddhist meditation as well as poetry at the Naropa Institute.

Music and dance in the United States also have been affected by East Asian thought, practices, and the migration of composers and choreographers. Most prominent among the American composers influenced by Asian philosophy and religion is John Cage, who delivered the Charles Eliot Norton Lectures at Harvard in 1988–89. His best-known composition, *4' 33"* (1952), consists of a pianist stepping on stage, sitting at the piano in silence for four minutes and thirty-three seconds—divided into three movements—and then walking off. Cage developed an interest in Buddhism in the 1930s and in the late 1940s studied Zen at Columbia University. In 1950 he discovered the *I Ching*. It gave him the idea for his "Chance" compositions, musical works created by using chance processes while the audience watched. The pieces were composed and played simultaneously. For example, in his "Music of Changes," performers used charts based on the *I Ching* and then tossed coins to determine pitch, duration, timbre, and dynamics. The scores would contain elements of randomness and would vary from performance to performance. The peak period of Cage's interest in Zen was the 1950s, when his New York loft became a salon for young poets and artists seeking inspiration for new approaches.[48] It was Cage who introduced the prize-winning composer Philip Glass to the *I Ching* and to Daoism, stimulating Glass's interest in the Asian literature and religion that have colored his own work.

The American music scene has also benefited from the presence of Asian-born composers such as Chou Wen-cheng, Bright Sheng, and Chen Yi, all originally from China. Chou came to the United States shortly after World War II and in 1949 composed *Landscapes,* based on traditional Chinese melodies. He taught composition at Columbia University for many years and, toward the end of his career, devoted himself to promoting artistic exchanges with the People's Republic of China. A string quartet recently composed by Sheng was declared a "major new contribution to the literature," although the reviewer complained that Sheng sold it to a Freer Gallery audience as a "silly mood piece with a chic Buddhist atmosphere."[49] Chen Yi recently won the prestigious $225,000 Charles Ives Living Prize of the American Academy of Arts and Letters for her compositions in which "Chinese and western influences and instrumentation mingle freely and colorfully."[50]

Contemporary dance in the United States is well seasoned with once-exotic Asian techniques. The Pilobolus Dance Theater of Connecticut recently collaborated with the Japanese *taiko* drummer Leonard Eto in a performance of *Tsu-Ku-Tsu,* which, unfortunately, was not very well received. Eto has performed with Bob Dylan, and his compositions were part of the sound track of several American films, including *The Lion King, J.F.K.,* and *The Thin Red Line.*[51] The Chinese choreographer Shen Pei now resides in St. Paul, Minnesota, where she is artistic director of the Chinese Dance Theater of Minnesota.[52] In Long Beach, California, Cambodian-born choreographer Sophiline Cheam Shapiro has retold Shakespeare's *Othello* as a classical Khmer dance to be shown in Pnom Penh; she also creates and promotes intercultural arts in her new home community.[53] Just as African and Latin rhythms changed American music and dance earlier in the nation's history, Asian influence was increasing as the twentieth century drew to a close.

A current that runs through much of this Asian influence on American culture is unquestionably Buddhism, which has become a major force in American life, both as Asian Buddhists migrate to the United States and as Euro and African Americans find in Buddhism the satisfaction and meaning they have not been able to find elsewhere.

Buddhism has existed in America for more than a century, brought over by early immigrants, but it has become a mass movement only in the last thirty years or so. There were an estimated four to six million Buddhists in the country in the year 2000, three-fourths of them in immigrant communities. At present, they constitute approximately 2 percent of the population of the United States, while American Jews constitute about 3 percent. Even conceding some overlap, there likely will be more Buddhists than Jews in America by mid-century. American Buddhism is already larger than many Protestant denominations.[54]

At the academic level, there are more than one hundred fifty scholars teaching and writing about Buddhism. At least two dozen universities have two or more specialists in Buddhist studies, and several, including Harvard, the University of Chicago, and the University of California at Berkeley, have been given endowments for chairs in Buddhist studies. One school, American University in Washington, D.C., has had a Buddhist chaplain.

In the very complex tapestry of Buddhism across the country, there are at least three readily discernible threads. First, there is the BCA, the organization of the Buddhist Churches of America, comprised largely of third-, fourth-, and fifth-generation Asian Americans, mostly Japanese. Its temples were established early in the twentieth century, and its members inherited their Buddhism. Before 1950, most Buddhists in the United States fell into this category. Today the BCA is the most fragile thread, facing declining membership and a high rate of outmarriage. Over the years it has become highly Americanized; it has adapted to American culture by having Sunday services, in English, and temple-sponsored basketball leagues.

The second thread—and the most exotic—is composed of non-Asian converts, primarily Caucasian, disproportionately Jewish, but with significant African American and Hispanic membership. Although a handful of converts could be found in America in the late nineteenth century, most of the convert community's roots go back only as far as the 1950s. In the 1960s, as part of the counterculture, Buddhist practices and ideas burst forth all over the country. This convert community is unquestionably strong today, but it remains to be seen whether it will survive the baby-boom generation.

The third thread is comprised of recent Asian immigrants and refugees, who started coming from Asia in large numbers when American immigration law changed in 1965—a critical point in American history to which I will return. Among these groups, Chinese Buddhism is the strongest, with separate ethnic temples for Koreans, Vietnamese, Thais, Cambodians, and Laotians. This is by far the largest category of Buddhists in the United States, constantly revitalized with new waves of immigrants, with a new "first generation." It is likely to be the dominant force in American Buddhism for the foreseeable future—and long afterward, if immigration law does not become more restrictive.

Most converts practice some form of Zen Buddhism or are members of the Soka Gakkai International. Converts include many celebrities: Tina Turner and bell hooks are probably the most prominent African American Buddhists. A list of Euro American celebrity Buddhists might begin with Phil Jackson, longtime coach of the World Champion Chicago Bulls who more recently led the Los Angeles Lakers to the 2000 NBA championship. An unusual figure in the sports world, who gives his star players books to read (he gave Shaq

O'Neal a book by Nietzsche), Jackson has a self-abnegating style that is presumed to come from his practice of Zen Buddhism.[55] Others might begin with Jerry Brown, erstwhile governor of California, presidential candidate, and current mayor of Oakland. If one stretches a bit and includes Tantric or Tibetan Buddhists, one can add Richard Gere, Philip Glass, Oliver Stone, Steve Seagal, and one or more of the "Beastie Boys."

It is evident that there always has been a small number of Americans interested in Eastern philosophy as part of their search for the meaning of life. For a few, Buddhism proved intellectually and spiritually attractive. But when we examine the 1950s and 1960s, we observe a radical change. Some of the broader and more intense interest in Buddhism in that period may have been a response to the terror of the emerging Cold War, to discomfort with what America seemed to represent in the 1950s. In addition, with the end of the American occupation of Japan, there was renewed interest in Japanese culture and a resumption of cultural exchanges between Japan and the United States.

Whatever the cause, there seemed to be more young people searching for meaning, and more of them finding Buddhism as an answer. Initially, the center of interest in Buddhism was New York City, most likely because of the charismatic D. T. Suzuki, who taught Buddhism at Columbia in the 1950s. Suzuki lectured around town, exciting a host of young intellectuals and Greenwich Village habitués, including Jack Kerouac and the Beat poets, who spread the word. At the same time, a small group of Japanese, mostly war brides, more widely scattered, were proselytizing for what became Soka Gakkai International—and they welcomed African Americans and Hispanics into their meetings.

By the 1960s, the counterculture was in full bloom. Meditation, chanting, and psychedelic drugs seemed to go well together, enabling people to gain a spiritual experience without having to go to a church or synagogue. It is evident that meditation and chanting, at least, have therapeutic value. Discontent with established institutions led more and more young Americans to experiment with versions of Buddhism—or what they perceived to be Buddhism. Many of these people began to study Buddhism seriously, with some going to Asia to enter monasteries and to work with great teachers.

A more recent phenomenon has been the spread of Buddhist practice among prison inmates. The Zen Mountain Monastery in Mount Tremper, New York, the Prison Daharma Network in Boulder, Colorado, the Buddhist Peace Fellowship in Berkeley, California, and the San Francisco Zen Center sponsor prison meditation groups and maintain contacts with prisoners across the country. Zen Mountain, which supports the Lotus Flower Sangha in a maximum security prison in Stormville, New York, is developing training manuals for inmates who want to begin meditation practice on their own.[56]

One major group in American Buddhism is the Insight Meditation Movement, formed in 1975 by three young people who had been trained in Southeast Asia in the 1960s: Sharon Salzberg, who studied in Burma as well as South Asia; Jack Kornfield, who started his studies while in the Peace Corps in Thailand; and Joseph Goldstein, who followed the same pattern. They teach a form of monastic meditation, which they call "awareness technique," designed to awaken and heal through Buddhist practices.

As the counterculture faded in the age of Ronald Reagan, a shortage of American-born teachers seemed likely, but it no longer mattered. After 1965, with the change in the immigration law, there has been a flood of *Asian* teachers to spread the word. The most important of these is Thich Nat Hanh, surpassed for veneration among Buddhists only by the Dalai Lama. It is these Asian teachers who are the best hope for the survival and growth of the convert community.

One obvious point is that as Buddhism has been adapted to American culture, to American values, it may have been watered down. There is certainly the danger of excessive interpretation. Often what we see is the spread of what might be described as "Zen-like" ideas. What emerges is Zen with American characteristics, much like baseball with Japanese characteristics—or China's socialist market economy. All of these are hybrids that have vitality as a result of successful adaptation to the host country's culture.

The dominant strains of Buddhism in America, however, are in the immigrant communities. These constitute a world very different from that of the converts. For the immigrants, the existence of Buddhist temples and the opportunity for Buddhist worship represent a means of preserving ethnic culture. As with earlier immigrant groups, the most recent arrivals tend to be the most traditional. Nonetheless, they are adapting to issues ranging from pressures for democratization and gender equality to modification of the traditional garments of Buddhist monks and nuns.

An amusing story of accommodation to local conditions occurred in St. Louis, where the monks of a Thai temple wore the traditional cotton robes of Southeast Asia. Their non-Buddhist neighbors feared the monks would freeze to death if they were in a car or bus that broke down in a midwestern winter storm and appealed to the monks' superiors to allow them to wear clothing like that of Christian or Jewish clergy. The appeal was denied, but a compromise was reached, authorizing the monks to wear thermal underwear, knit hats, and socks with their sandals—the Americanization of Thai Buddhism.

The Laotian temple Wat Lao Buddavong Sala, built near the village of Catlett, Virginia, in 1991, has become one of the nation's great Fourth of July weekend attractions. Every year, in celebration of Independence Day, the temple grounds become a Southeast Asian market, drawing 20,000 visitors who donate five dollars apiece to have an opportunity to eat, enjoy traditional music and dance—and pray to the Buddha. The Independence Day festivities now surpass in size, if not piety, the annual rites for the Buddhist New Year.[57]

Perhaps the most famous—or notorious—Buddhist temple in America, as well as the largest immigrant temple and monastery, is Hsi Lai, near Los Angeles, part of an order founded in Taiwan. The order, Fou Guang Shan, also known as the International Buddhist Progress Society, has nineteen temples in the United States. Most of those who worship at Hsi Lai are from Taiwan, but the temple is determined to attract Euro Americans, to Americanize Buddhism. On Sundays, it holds classes conducted in English for potential converts. Nearby it has built Hsi Lai University, offering degrees in Buddhist studies, and in Whittier it has built a three-story pagoda. In 1996, demonstrating that Hsi Lai had adapted to and been accepted by American culture, Vice President Al Gore attended a luncheon at Hsi Lai—at which $55,000 in illegal foreign contributions were made to the Democratic National Committee. Gore has had ample reason to regret the temple fund-raiser, but the temple itself seems to have recovered from the very American transgression to which it played host.[58]

The critical question is one that earlier religious traditions in America confronted: can a strong pan-Buddhist national organization emerge that can not only bridge the gap between the various ethnic traditions of immigrant Buddhists, but also that between immigrants and converts? Buddhism will very likely continue to change as it adapts to the dominant culture, as immigrant worshipers and their children assimilate—but the dominant culture is also changing, becoming more hospitable to Buddhism. It is still too early to predict the outcome, but it is apparent that Buddhism has a firm foothold in the United States, that it will grow stronger in the years ahead, and that it will strengthen the challenge to those who would call America a *Christian* nation.

Most of this cultural transfer from East Asia to the United States mirrors cultural transfer from the United States to East Asia, at least in terms of popular culture. Two cultures meet and take from each other whatever appears useful, whatever seems likely to improve the quality of life. But just as there is an asymmetry in the movement of political culture between America and Asia, there is also a very different kind of cultural transfer that has been unidirectional and has worked to the advantage of the United States, which has gained enormously by opening its doors to immigrants and refugees from East Asia. The freedom, power, and wealth that have made American culture attractive to Asians seeking ways to improve life in their homeland have also served as a magnet drawing millions of Asians to the shores of the United States.

Asian Americans have been a part of American life since the nineteenth century, and they have been living testimony to the power of racism in American culture. We should never forget the various Oriental exclusion laws, the segregation of Asians, and the discrimination against them, culminating in the internment of Japanese Americans during World War II. Even as late as the 1950s, Southern political leaders opposed admitting Hawaii to statehood because the majority of its population was not white and would likely send Asian Americans to Congress.

Hawaii is, of course, an exceptional story. The white planters who succeeded in persuading Washington to annex the islands in 1898 had been importing Chinese, Portuguese, and Japanese laborers in the last half of the nineteenth century. By 1900 the Japanese were the largest ethnic group in Hawaii. Attempting to weaken the bargaining power of the Japanese, the planters conspired with Horace Allen in Korea to bring in Korean workers. In 1905 the government of Japan, having gained control of Korea, stopped the migration of Koreans, but the planters simply switched to recruiting Filipinos. Even when U.S. immigration laws, applied to Hawaii, kept other Asians out, Filipinos, as American subjects, continued to come.[59]

The wealthy and powerful planters continued to control the islands until the 1950s. Nisei veterans of World War II, members of the famed 442nd Division, used the GI bill to gain the education the planters had denied them and then attained leadership positions in government and politics. They seized control of the Democratic Party, and in 1954 they won control of Hawaii's legislature. They sent a Chinese American, Hiram Fong, to the U.S. Senate in 1959, immediately after the granting of statehood. Daniel Inouye became the new state's first representative and the first Japanese American congressman, subsequently winning election to the U.S.

Senate in 1962. In 1974, George Ariyoshi became the first Japanese American elected governor. In the 1990s, nearly two-thirds of the population of Hawaii was of Asian-Pacific ancestry.

But Hawaii, dominated since statehood by Asian Americans, has been considered an anomaly—Pacific islands distant from mainstream America, acquired under dubious circumstances, achieving statehood largely because colonial rule was no longer feasible and because cutting the strategically valuable territory loose was perceived by those in Washington to be too dangerous. My focus here is on the mainland of the United States, the lower forty-eight states, and how Asian Americans are rapidly gaining influence there. That story begins in the second half of the twentieth century, especially the last thirty-five years of that century.

Laws prohibiting Chinese immigration and citizenship were repealed during World War II. The Chinese were, after all, allies of the United States, and Americans shamelessly allowed a mere 105 of them to enter the United States each year. In 1952, embarrassed by national origin quotas for would-be immigrants and by the evident racism that undermined Washington's Cold War efforts to win friends and influence people in Asia, the U.S. government lifted the exclusionary restriction on other Asians. But immigration from the nineteen countries in the Asian Pacific region was limited to a total of two thousand annually. This trickle, with the addition of Japanese and Korean war brides, brought the total of Americans of Asian descent in the United States, including Hawaii, to a minuscule one million in 1965, most of them American-born.

In 1965, for reasons having nothing to do with Asia, Congress changed American immigration law. Thereafter, a quota of twenty thousand was allotted to *each* country of the Eastern Hemisphere, regardless of size. In addition, an unlimited number of immigrant visas was granted to the immediate relatives of U.S. citizens, and to a number of preferred groups, such as refugees from communism—presumably Cubans and Soviet Jews. To the astonishment of lawmakers, hundreds of thousands of Asians poured into the country. By 1990, the number of residents of Asian ancestry jumped to seven million, a 700 percent increase. There are more than ten million at the beginning of the twenty-first century. By 2050, 10 percent of "We the People" will be of Asian ancestry—most, but not all, from East Asia.[60] Given the imperfections of the "melting pot," these new immigrants are contributing mightily to the diversification of American culture. A smaller percentage of Americans will be white, or Christian, or Atlanticists. The critical point is that American identity has changed.

And it is changing in another way. The 1990 census indicated that 31 percent, nearly a third, of Asian Americans marry interracially. More recent estimates suggest that this is true of more than half of Japanese Americans. Some specialists in cultural contact and cultural transer refer to the outcome as "hybridization." By these intermarriages, we have developed uniquely American hybrids, of whom the most famous in the year 2000 is undoubtedly Tiger Woods, the great golfer, who is African American and Thai. As these "hybrids" become increasingly commonplace, they are less likely to experience the kind of identity crisis that troubled Noguchi.[61]

We are all familiar with the reports of Asian Americans as the "model minority," with specific reference to their impressive educational and economic achievements—often implicitly offered as an invidious contrast to the performance of African Americans. Obviously, not all fit that stereotype. Statistically, the median income of Asian American families *is* above that for Euro and African Americans, but there are also more Asian American families, especially Cambodian and Laotian refugees, *below* the poverty line than any other ethnic group in the United States. Nonetheless, the educational achievements of Asian American families are striking. Today they constitute 4 to 5 percent of the population, but they constitute approximately 19 percent of the student body at Harvard, 30 percent at MIT, and 40 percent at UCLA and the University of California at Berkeley.

Asian Americans are the fastest-growing population group, generally the most affluent, and the best educated. They outspend every other ethnic group for computers, insurance, and long distance calls. As one might expect, Madison Avenue has noticed and is directing advertising toward Asian Americans, "diversity's darlings."[62] Marketers face a difficult problem, however, because this is not a monolithic group: there are significant ethnic differences. The *New York Times* ran a Chinese-language ad campaign in New York and California in 1999. It is preparing to run one in New York in Korean. AT&T markets in Cantonese as well as Mandarin Chinese, in Japanese, Korean, Vietnamese, and Tagalog. Many leading firms, including Apple Computers, Hallmark, MCI WorldCom., Charles Schwab, and the Seagrams Company, run ads in Asian languages. Perhaps most striking is the fact that the U.S. Census Bureau's advertising campaign for the year 2000 questionnaire devoted 13 percent of its budget to attempting to reach Asian Americans, with ads in Chinese, Korean, Tagalog, and Vietnamese.

Several articles have been published recently that extol the virtues of Asian men. For many years the tendency, at least in Hollywood, was to view Asian women as exotically beautiful, mysterious, and sexy, while males of Asian ancestry lacked comparable cachet, too often portrayed as androgynous or sexless. But the portrait has changed. The *Wall Street Journal, Washington Post,* and *Newsweek* have all run articles with titles like "Why Asian Guys Are on a Roll" and "Asian Males Are In." Advertisers like them because they are perceived as affluent, and Hollywood has pushed Asian actors like Chow Yun Fat and Jet Li as action heroes. According to *Newsweek,* Asian men will be the next "trophy boyfriends" for the smart set.[63]

One source of the wealth of Asian Americans has been

their replication of the role played by the Chinese diaspora in Southeast Asia, both as entrepreneurs and as central figures in trade between China and their countries of residence. As trade across the Pacific has boomed for the United States, especially with China, and as Asian nations have sought American technology, migrants from Asia to America have been important facilitators. Many American organizations, both business and governmental, use Asian Americans to represent them in their ancestral countries. McDonnell Douglas, for example, hired the retired general John Fugh, a Chinese American, to oversee its operations in China, and the state of Maryland employed a Chinese émigré to open and direct its office in Shanghai.

American society has had to adjust to the influx of Asians in many different ways. Public schools across the country, but especially on both coasts, have been forced to accommodate children who speak little or no English. Libraries are opening foreign-language sections for patrons for whom reading English is a struggle. The Wheaton Regional Library in Montgomery County, Maryland, provides library card application forms written entirely in Chinese.[64] Cable television offers programming in several Asian languages, including news broadcasts from Beijing and Taibei. In the Washington region alone there are three Korean-language daily newspapers and a half-dozen weeklies. In many areas, church services are offered in Asian languages, especially for Korean

Protestants and Vietnamese Catholics. In June, 2000, a Korean-born minister was elected moderator of the Presbyterian Church (U.S.A.), the highest office in America's largest Presbyterian denomination.[65] And Vietnamese Americans are providing a disproportionately high percentage of priests and nuns for the Catholic Church in the United States, at a time when fewer and fewer Euro Americans are called to these vocations.[66]

Of course, some of the immigrants from East Asia have not been assets to the United States. Problems with transnational crime have increased, although Asian groups seem to have been overshadowed by the Russian Mafia. Smuggling of illegal immigrants and the enslavement of some of these has been traced to Chinese and Thai families operating in the United States. Asian organized crime groups hijack cars in the United States to sell in China, Taiwan, and Hong Kong and bring guns and drugs back to America. They extort money from Chinese Americans for relatives kidnapped in Asia.[67]

Concerns about the activities of the Reverend Sun Myung Moon and his Unification Church have continued to reverberate, long after his conviction, imprisonment, and departure from American shores. Moon sent his first missionary to the United States in 1959 and moved his base there in the early 1970s; he organized a seminary in Tarrytown, New York, in the mid-1970s. Membership increased rapidly in America, as did the church's success as a business conglomerate. Apprehensions about the church as a cult also increased as his followers, the "Moonies," were perceived widely as dupes of a charismatic leader. A congressional investigation in the late 1970s reported that Reverend Moon had ties to Korean intelligence. In 1983 he was jailed for tax evasion, despite the efforts of the ACLU on his behalf. Church membership declined sharply in the 1990s, but discomfort remains over its ownership of the ultra-conservative *Washington Times,* launched in 1982, its purchase of the University of Bridgeport in 1992, and its purchase of the wire service U.P.I. in 2000.[68]

The last point I want to raise is the possible impact on American foreign policy of this striking increase in the Asianization of the American people. Foreign governments have attempted to influence American policy since the beginning of the republic. The "China Lobby," which worked on behalf of Jiang Jieshi and the Guomindang, was remarkably successful in the 1940s and 1950s. But a foreign state has a very different kind of leverage in the United States when it is presumed by American politicians to have a large number of supporters among American voters, as for example the power Israel enjoys in its dealings with U.S. officials. Sometimes the presence of a significant voting bloc that is hostile to a foreign government affects American policy, as in the case of Cuban-American antipathy toward Castro. And there are also cases of Americans whose loyalty is questioned because of their ethnicity or political beliefs, as was the case with Japanese

Americans during World War II, American communists during the Cold War, and, most recently, Chinese Americans, as relations between the United States and the People's Republic totter on the brink of unpleasantness. A quarter of a century ago, Nathan Glazer and Daniel Patrick Moynihan argued that the immigration process was the single most important determinant of American foreign policy—that policy responded to ethnic composition.[69]

There have also been recent instances in which Asian governments, Taiwan and Korea, for example, harassed—even murdered—dissidents who emigrated or were living in exile in the United States. Taiwan security forces were implicated in the 1984 murder of Henry Liu, a naturalized American citizen living in California, who had the temerity to write a biography critical of Jiang Jingguo.[70] The "Koreagate" scandal of 1976 resulted from revelations that 115 members of Congress had been accepting favors from the Seoul government totaling five hundred thousand to one million dollars per year. The Korean Central Intelligence Agency was attempting to deflect criticism of its efforts to intimidate Korean Americans and of Seoul's human rights policies.

In these many different ways, Asian Americans, innocently or otherwise, can get caught up in the politics of their ancestral homelands, as was true of the men and women who came across the Atlantic in centuries past. But in recent years, Asian Americans have been organizing to play a more active role in

American politics and in the shaping of U.S. foreign policy. It appears to have been the African American struggle for civil rights in the 1960s that prompted Asian Americans to recognize their ethnic identity and set the pattern for advocacy of their rights as well. African American studies programs on university campuses were soon followed by Asian American studies programs, sometimes forced upon reluctant administrators by student activists. In 2000, a pair of Filipino American sisters led a successful five-year battle to persuade the University of Maryland to offer the first such program in the Washington-Baltimore area.[71]

Advocacy groups, often reflecting the diversity of Asian Americans, sprang up to speak for the concerns of Chinese or Koreans or Filipinos in the United States. Frequently activists found that the most effective way of mobilizing their ethnic community was by focusing on political causes, especially human-rights issues, in their country of origin.[72] Taiwanese in America organized for independence and an end to mainlander domination of their island. Koreans demanded that the U.S. government promote democracy in Korea. Filipinos called for an end to the Marcos dictatorship. After the Tiananmen massacre, Chinese in the United States lobbied for sanctions against the Beijing regime. Of course, the Washington embassies of the various East Asian countries attempted to mobilize supporters of their respective regimes residing in the United States.[73]

By the 1990s, Asian Americans had been energized and had become an important force in mainstream American politics. In Congress, representatives of Asian ancestry were sufficient in number to form an Asian Pacific Caucus. Prominent Chinese Americans, including Bette Bao Lord, Yo-Yo Ma, I. M. Pei, Chang-lin Tien, and the ethically-challenged Democratic fund raiser John Huang, formed the Committee of 100 to oversee media and government performance in dealing with China, and to lobby on issues of American policy toward China.[74] Asian Americans working for the federal government organized the Asian Pacific Federal Foreign Affairs Council, with the stated mission of "active involvement in US foreign affairs."[75] In 2000, several Asian American organizations called for boycotts of federal laboratories to protest the treatment of Wen Ho Lee, a former U.S.-government-employed scientist accused of mishandling nuclear secrets.[76] A national coalition of Asian American leaders, angered by what they perceive as anti-Asian ethnic profiling, has formed a political action committee, the 80–20 Initiative, designed to get out the Asian American vote, and to maximize their leverage by delivering 80 percent of that vote to the political party that is most likely to serve their agenda.[77]

Many Chinese-born scholars, such as Huang Yasheng of Harvard and Pei Minxin of the Carnegie Institute, frequently appear on television or publish policy-relevant articles in major newspapers and journals. A leading academic specialist in Asian American studies, L. Ling-chi Wang, has contended that Chinese in the United States are having a "phenomenal influence" on American diplomacy.[78] In 2000 a Taiwan-born congressman, vice-chair of the Congressional Asian Pacific Caucus, opposed "permanent normal trade relations" (PNTR) with China because of its human-rights record. Obviously, Americans of Chinese ancestry are divided, especially on the Taiwan issue, but also between older immigrants from Guangdong and more recent arrivals from Fujian. And Chinese in America may differ from other Asian Americans on a wide range of issues. The important point is that Asian Americans generally and Chinese in particular are politically active and influence public opinion, congressional committees, and the electoral process.

One reason for the increasing attention given to the views of Asian Americans in recent years by the Department of State, the Pentagon, and the Congress is, unquestionably, the numbers—the millions of Asian immigrants who have come to the United States since 1965. At least as important is the fact that Asian immigrants have a much higher rate of naturalization than immigrants from other parts of the world: two and a half to three times that of immigrants from Europe and twenty times that of those from Mexico.[79] Asian immigrants also tend to be better educated and more likely to vote. As a Pentagon specialist in Asian affairs noted, California is enormously important in U.S. domestic politics—and

Asian Americans are increasingly influential in that state's elections.[80]

In my discussion of the international politics of East Asia in the "American century," I argued that East Asia is better off today than it would have been without the role played by the United States in the region in the twentieth century. I concede readily that other analysts might disagree with that conclusion. But I see little likelihood that reasonable men and women would disagree with my insistence that the United States is also better off. Americans have paid a heavy price for some of that contact, and some of the cost, as in Vietnam, was unnecessary, even immoral.[81] Nonetheless, Americans have been enormously enriched by the encounter, primarily by the Asians who have come to be a part of the American people. Asians have given the United States architects and artists, film directors, choreographers, musicians, novelists,[82] and scholars, as well as doctors, nurses, engineers, computer nerds—and even a president of that most august body, the American Historical Association.

As we begin the twenty-first century, the United States, its people, and their culture cannot be considered products exclusively of Western civilization. The extensive—and intensive—contact with East Asia in the previous hundred or so years has changed America dramatically. Even if Asians stop coming to our shores, even if those already here were to be assimilated at approximately the same rate and to the same extent as were the Europeans who came before them, the integration of Asian culture with American culture could not be undone easily. And just as the Asians among us and our contacts with Asia have led us to change our ideas about what constitutes art, what is edible, what an American looks like—our habits, values, and even our identity—they have also changed our perception of the relative importance of Europe and Asia, our conception of economic, political, and military strategies appropriate for the future.

Perhaps one day American power and wealth will diminish to the point where few in Asia seek to emulate the United States, when the Americanization of Asia and fear of American cultural imperialism will be forgotten. But the impact of Asia on America in the twentieth century almost certainly will persist, thanks to that asymmetrical flow of migrants across the Pacific.

NOTES

1. THE STRUGGLE FOR DOMINANCE IN EAST ASIA

1. Gong, *The Standard of "Civilization" in International Society* (Oxford: Clarendon Press, 1984).

2. See his *After Imperialism: The Search for a New Order in the Far East, 1921–1931* (Cambridge, Mass.: Harvard University Press, 1965).

3. Borg's Bancroft-Prize-winning *The United States and the Far Eastern Crisis of 1933–1938* (Cambridge, Mass.: Harvard University Press, 1964) conclusively eliminates concern for China or its market as motivation for American policy. Heinrichs' *Threshold of War: Franklin D. Roosevelt and American Entry into World War II* (New York: Oxford University Press, 1988) points to the perceived need to deter Japan from attacking the Soviet Union as it tottered on the brink of defeat in the autumn of 1941. See also Warren I. Cohen, "The Issue of China in Japanese-American Relations, 1931–1941," in Hosoya Chihiro et al. (eds.), *The Pacific War* (Tokyo: University of Tokyo Press, 1993) [in Japanese], 69–86.

4. Schroeder, *The Axis Alliance and Japanese-American Relations, 1941* (Ithaca: Cornell University Press, 1958); Russett, *No*

Clear and Present Danger: A Skeptical View of the U.S. Entry into World War II (New York: Harper & Row, 1972).

5. Dower, "Occupied Japan and the American Lake, 1945–1950," in Edward Friedman and Mark Selden (eds.), *America's Asia: Dissenting Essays on Asian-American Relations* (New York: Pantheon, 1971), 146–206; Cumings, *Parallax Visions: Making Sense of American-East Asian Relations at the End of the Century* (Durham: Duke University Press, 1999); Johnson, *Blowback: The Costs and Consequences of American Empire* (New York: Metropolitan Books, 2000).

6. Barbara W. Tuchman's *Stilwell and the American Experience in China, 1911–1945* (New York: Macmillan, 1970) is the most accessible account of American disillusionment with Jiang's China.

7. See the highly respected work of Bruce Cumings, *The Origins of the Korean War,* 2 vols. (Princeton: Princeton University Press, 1981, 1990).

8. Fairbank, *China: The People's Middle Kingdom and the U.S.A.* (Cambridge, Mass.: Harvard University Press, 1967), 101.

9. Smith, *International History of the War in Vietnam* (London: Macmillan, 1983, 1985).

10. William Burr (ed.), *The Kissinger Transcripts: The Top Secret Talks with Beijing and Moscow* (New York: New Press, 1998).

11. See the article by Simei Qing, "The Eisenhower Administration and Changes in Western Embargo Policy against China," in Warren I. Cohen and Akira Iriye (eds.), *The Great Powers in East Asia, 1953–1960* (New York: Columbia University Press, 1990), 121–142.

12. Tucker, "John Foster Dulles and the Taiwan Roots of the 'Two Chinas' Policy," in Richard Immerman (ed.), *John Foster Dulles and the Diplomacy of the Cold War* (Princeton: Princeton University Press, 1989), 236–262; Warren I. Cohen, *Dean Rusk* (Totowa, N.J.: Cooper Square Press, 1980), 85.

13. The fullest discussion of China's role in Vietnam, based largely on Chinese documents, is Qiang Zhai's *China and the Vietnam Wars, 1950–1975* (Chapel Hill: University of North Carolina Press, 2000).

14. Burr, *Kissinger Transcripts.*

15. Deng to Nixon and Kissinger in 1989. Quoted in Harry Harding, *Fragile Relationship: The United States and China since 1972* (Washington, D.C.: Brookings Institution, 1992), 251.

16. Thomas E. Ricks, "For Pentagon, Asia Moving to Forefront," *Washington Post,* May 26, 2000, 1, 26.

17. *The Paradox of China's Post-Mao Reforms* (Cambridge, Mass.: Harvard University Press, 1999).

18. See Michael J. Green, "The Forgotten Player," *National Interest,* 60 (Summer 2000), 42–49.

2. THE AMERICANIZATION OF EAST ASIA

1. Quoted in Aviad E. Raz, *Riding the Black Ship: Japan and Tokyo Disneyland* (Cambridge, Mass.: Harvard University Asia Center, 1999), 194.

2. Edward Wong, "New York Attitude Packaged for Tokyo," *New York Times,* June 24, 2000, A15.

3. Ian Buruma, *God's Dust: A Modern Asian Journey* (New York: Noonday, 1993), 127.

4. Akira Iriye, *Pacific Estrangement: Japanese and American Expansion, 1897–1911* (Cambridge, Mass.: Harvard University Press, 1972), 26.

5. Gluck, *Japan's Modern Myths: Ideology in the Late Meiji Period* (Princeton: Princeton University Press), 162, 207.

6. Mitsuko Iriye, introduction to her translation of Nagai Kafu, *American Stories* (New York: Columbia University Press, 2000), xxii.

7. R. David Arkush and Leo O. Lee (eds.), *Land Without Ghosts: Chinese Impressions of America from the Mid-Nineteenth Century to the Present* (Berkeley: University of California Press, 1989), 8–10.

8. Cited in Frederick Wakeman, Jr., *History and Will: Philosophical Perspectives of Mao Tse-tung's Thought* (Berkeley: University of California Press, 1973), 150.

9. Dunch, "Piety, Patriotism, Progress: Chinese Protestants in Fuzhou Society and the Making of a Modern China, 1857–1927," unpublished dissertation, Yale University, 1996, 214–226. I am grateful to Paul A. Cohen for calling the manuscript to my attention.

10. Vipan Chandra, *Imperialism, Resistance, and Reform in Late Nineteenth-Century Korea: Enlightenment and the Independence Club* (Berkeley: Center for Korean Studies, University of California, 1988).

11. Mark Philip Bradley, *Imagining Vietnam and America: The Making of Postcolonial Vietnam, 1919–1950* (Chapel Hill: University of North Carolina Press, 2000).

12. Silverberg, "Constructing a New Cultural History of Prewar Japan," in Masao Miyoshi and H. D. Harootunian, *Japan in the World* (Durham, N.C.: Duke University Press, 1993), 115–143.

13. David T. Roy, *Kuo Mo-jo: The Early Years* (Cambridge, Mass.: Harvard University Press, 1971); see also Leo Ou-fan Lee, *The Romantic Generation of Modern Chinese Writers* (Cambridge, Mass.: Harvard University Press, 1973), 184, 187, 190, 195–196.

14. Quoted in Joseph R. Levenson, *Confucian China and Its Modern Fate: A Trilogy* (Berkeley: University of California Press, 1968), I, 111.

15. Paul A. Cohen, *Discovering History in China: American Historical Writing on the Recent Chinese Past* (New York: Columbia University Press, 1984), 13.

16. Buruma, *God's Dust,* 60.

17. Ginny Parker, "Starbucks Finds Asia a Vast, Thirsty Market," *Toronto Globe and Mail,* May 29, 2000, B6.

18. *Washington Post,* March 19, 2000, G2.

19. Nichole M. Christian, "Spirits Soar as Japanese Sing Gospel in Harlem," *New York Times,* September 18, 2000, A25.

20. Buruma, *God's Dust,* 45.

21. Gia Kourlas, "Modern and Chinese: No Oxymoron," *New York Times,* February 25, 2001, AR 39.

22. Silverberg, "Constructing a New Cultural History," 140.

23. John Clark, "Modernity in Japanese Painting," *Art History,* 9 (1986), 213–231; Warren I. Cohen, *East Asian Art and American Culture* (New York: Columbia University Press, 1992), 27–28.

24. Vicki Goldberg, "In Japan, Pathfinders Romancing the Camera," *New York Times,* October 1, 2000, AR 35–36.

25. *New York Times,* October 3, 1999, II, 41–42.

26. See Joan Lebold Cohen, *The New Chinese Painting, 1949–1986* (New York: Harry N. Abrams, 1987), 6–7.

27. Michael Sullivan, "Art and Reality in Twentieth Century Chinese Painting," in Mayching Kao (ed.), *Twentieth Century Chinese Painting* (Hong Kong: Oxford University Press, 1988), 18.

28. Garrett, *Social Reformers in Urban China: The Chinese Y.M.C.A., 1895–1926* (Cambridge, Mass.: Harvard University Press, 1970), 100.

29. Agence France Press, March 31, 2000. A year later, as a "good-will gesture," the Chinese government relented and allowed Wang to play part of the season with Dallas. *New York Times,* March 17, 2001, B19.

30. Smith, *Japan: A Reinterpretation* (New York: Pantheon Books, 1997), p. 295.

31. Whiting, *The Chrysanthemum and the Bat* (Tokyo: The

Permanent Press, 1977), and *You Gotta Have Wa* (New York: Vintage, 1990).

32. Whiting, *You Gotta Have Wa*.

33. Brannen, "'Bwana Mickey'": Constructing Cultural Consumption at Tokyo Disneyland," in Joseph J. Tobin (ed.), *Remade in Japan: Everyday Life and Consumer Taste in a Changing Society* (New Haven: Yale University Press, 1992), 219.

34. Raz, *Riding the Black Ship*, 3, 6.

35. Ibid., 153, 200.

36. Watson (ed.), *Golden Arches East: McDonald's in East Asia* (Stanford: Stanford University Press, 1997).

37. Watson, "China's Big Mac Attack," *Foreign Affairs*, 79 (May/June 2000), 120–134.

38. Jun Jing (ed.), *Feeding China's Little Emperors: Food, Children, and Social Change* (Stanford: Stanford University Press, 2000).

39. Lozada, "Globalized Childhood? Kentucky Fried Chicken in China," in Jing (ed.), *Feeding China's Little Emperors*, 114–134.

40. Wang, *The Chinese Overseas: From Earthbound China to the Quest for Autonomy* (Cambridge, Mass.: Harvard University Press, 2000), 94.

41. Quoted by Edmund Capon, "A Sense of Unreality: Painting in the People's Republic of China," in Kao (ed.), *Twentieth Century Chinese Painting*, 169.

42. Cohen, *China and Christianity: The Missionary Movement and the Growth of Chinese Antiforeignism, 1860–1870* (Cambridge, Mass.: Harvard University Press, 1963).

43. The story of Allen's activities in Korea is told in Fred Harvey Harrington, *God, Mammon, and the Japanese: Dr. Horace N. Allen and Korean-American Relations, 1884–1905* (Madison: University of Wisconsin Press, 1966).

44. James Huntley Grayson, *Korea: A Religious History* (Oxford:

Clarendon Press, 1989); Gil Soo Han, *Social Sources of Church Growth: Korean Churches in the Homeland and Overseas* (Lanham, Md.: University Press of America, 1994).

45. Donald N. Clark, "History and Religion in Modern Korea: The Case of Protestant Christianity," in Lewis R. Lancaster and Richard K. Payne, *Religion and Society in Contemporary Korea* (Berkeley: Institute of East Asian Studies, 1997), 169–213.

46. Han, *History of Korea* (Seoul: Eul-Yoo Publishing Company, 1970), 458.

47. Korea Society, *Christianity in Korea: An Exploration of Its Unique Development* (1998), 10.

48. Ki-baik Lee, *A New History of Korea* (Cambridge, Mass.: Harvard University Press, 1984), 338.

49. Jessie Gregory Lutz, *China and the Christian Colleges, 1850–1950* (Ithaca: Cornell University Press, 1971).

50. Garrett, *Social Reformers in Urban China,* 120–121.

51. Parker's story is told beautifully in Edward V. Gulick, *Peter Parker and the Opening of China* (Cambridge, Mass.: Harvard University Press, 1973).

52. See Mary Brown Bullock, *An American Transplant: The Rockefeller Foundation and Peking Union Medical College* (Berkeley: University of California Press, 1980), and Warren I. Cohen, *The Chinese Connection: Roger S. Greene, Thomas W. Lamont, George E. Sokolsky and American–East Asian Relations* (New York: Columbia University Press, 1978), 32–40, 91–93, 146–147, 195–197.

53. Charles W. Hayford, *To the People: James Yen and Village China* (New York: Columbia University Press, 1990); see also Ka-che Yip, *Health and National Reconstruction in Nationalist China: The Development of Modern Health Services, 1928–1937* (Ann Arbor: AAS Monograph Series, no. 50, 1995).

54. Randall E. Stross, *The Stubborn Earth: American Agricultur-

alists on Chinese Soil, 1898–1937 (Berkeley: University of California Press, 1986), judges Buck harshly. For a more sympathetic account see James C. Thomson, Jr., *While China Faced West: American Reformers in Nationalist China, 1928–1937* (Cambridge, Mass.: Harvard University Press, 1969). Both hold Jiang responsible for inadequate support of the reform programs, but Stross argues that Buck and his colleagues should have known better than to expect the kind of support they needed—that they lacked a realistic understanding of the political and social milieu in which they were operating.

55. Nancy Bernkopf Tucker, *Taiwan, Hong Kong, and the United States, 1945–1992* (New York: Twayne, 1994), 55.

56. M. Searle Bates, "The Theology of American Missionaries in China, 1900–1950," in John K. Fairbank (ed.), *The Missionary Enterprise in China and America* (Cambridge, Mass.: Harvard University Press, 1974), 135–158.

57. Michael H. Hunt, in his "East Asia in Henry Luce's 'American Century,'" *Diplomatic History,* 23 (Spring 1999), 324, estimates total Filipino deaths at about 800,000, or one out of every ten Filipinos.

58. May, *Social Engineering in the Philippines: The Aims, Execution, and Impact of American Colonial Policy, 1900–1913* (Westport, Conn.: Greenwood Press, 1980), 17.

59. Fallows, "A Damaged Culture," *Atlantic,* 260 (November 1987), 49–58.

60. Renato Constantino, *Neocolonial Identity and Counter-Consciousness: Essays on Cultural Decolonization* (London: Merlin Press, 1978), especially 64–66.

61. Karnow, *In Our Image: America's Empire in the Philippines* (New York: Ballantine Books, 1989), preface, unpaginated.

62. Constantino, *Neocolonial Identity and Counter-Consciousness,* 76–78.

63. Buruma, *God's Dust,* 94, 85.

64. Dower, *Embracing Defeat: Japan in the Wake of World War II* (New York: Norton, 1999); see also his *Empire and Aftermath: Yoshida Shigeru and the Japanese Experience, 1878–1954* (Cambridge, Mass.: Council on East Asian Relations, Harvard University, 1979).

65. Dower, *Embracing Defeat,* 84.

66. Erlich, "Erasing and Refocusing: Two Films of the Occupation," in Mark Sandler, *The Confusion Era: Art and Culture of Japan during the Allied Occupation, 1945–1952* (Washington, D.C.: Sackler Gallery, 1997).

67. Comments of Marlene Mayo in conference transcript published as Thomas W. Burkman (ed.), *The Occupation of Japan: Arts and Culture* (Norfolk: General Douglas MacArthur Foundation, 1988), 52, 69.

68. Dower, *Embracing Defeat,* 138.

69. For a superb biography of Grew, see Waldo H. Heinrichs, Jr., *American Ambassador: Joseph C. Grew and the Development of the United States Diplomatic Tradition* (Boston: Little, Brown, 1966); see also Dower, *Empire and Aftermath,* p. 105, and Oliver Kunz, *Why the American Century?* (Chicago: University of Chicago Press, 1998), 165ff.

70. Dower, *Empire and Aftermath,* 561.

71. See Buruma, *God's Dust,* 231, and his review of Dower, *Embracing Defeat,* "MacArthur's Children," in *New York Review of Books,* October 21, 1999, 33–37.

72. Woo-Cumings, "Market Dependency in U.S.–East Asian Relations," in Arif Dirlik (ed.), *What Is in a Rim? Critical Perspectives*

on the Pacific Region Idea, 2nd ed. (Lanham: Rowman and Little-field, 1998), 171–175.

3. THE ASIANIZATION OF AMERICA

1. See A. Owen Aldridge, *The Dragon and the Eagle: The Presence of China in the American Enlightenment* (Detroit: Wayne State University Press, 1993).

2. Derk Bodde, "Henry A. Wallace and the Ever-Normal Granary," *Far Eastern Quarterly,* 5 (1946), 411–426.

3. Vogel, *Japan as Number One: Lessons for America* (Cambridge, Mass.: Harvard University Press, 1979).

4. Fallows, "Containing Japan," *The Atlantic* (May 1989) is the most accessible item in the "revisionist" arsenal; see also William S. Dietrich, *In the Shadow of the Rising Sun: The Political Roots of American Economic Decline* (University Park, Pa.: Pennsylvania State University Press, 1991).

5. Jeffrey K. Liker, W. Mark Fruin, and Paul S. Adler, *Remade in America: Transplanting and Transforming Japanese Management Systems* (New York: Oxford University Press, 1999), preface.

6. Paul Cohen, "The Asymmetry in Intellectual Relations Between China and the West in the Twentieth Century," unpublished paper presented at a conference in Taibei, January 2000. He notes that a leading Chinese scholar, Zi Zhongyun, has argued the same point in a paper specifically focused on Chinese-American relations.

7. William Woodward, "America as a Culture, II: A Fourfold Heritage," *Journal of American Culture,* 11 (Spring 1988), 30.

8. Fourth edition (New York: Oxford University Press, 1999).

9. A. O. Scott, "A Year That Was Very Good. Or Very Bad," *New York Times,* December 31, 2000, II: 11.

10. David Thomson, "A Master Returns to His Realm," *New York Times,* October 8, 2000, II: 11.

11. Laura Winters, "Jarmusch Still Fills the Role of Favorite Outsider," *New York Times,* February 27, 2000, AR 21.

12. Elvis Mitchell, "Hip-Hop Joins Martial Arts but Lets Plot Muscle In," *New York Times,* March 22, 2000, B3.

13. A. O. Scott, "New Age Meets Old West in a Multicultural Farce," *New York Times,* May 26, 2000, B12.

14. Hagedorn, "Asian Women in Film: No Joy, No Luck," *Ms.* (January/February 1994), 74–79.

15. Tung, "Asian 'It' Girls Say So Long, Dragon Lady," *New York Times,* May 21, 2000, 9: 1. See Alan James Frutkin, "The Faces in the Glass Are Rarely Theirs," *New York Times,* December 24, 2000, AR 31 for a discussion of TV roles for Asian Americans that notes the relative absence of male roles.

16. Don Shewey, "A Troupe That Sought an Asian-American Role," *New York Times,* March 4, 2001, II: 7.

17. Stanley Karnow, "Year in, year out, those eateries keep eggrolling along," *Smithsonian,* 24 (January 1994), 86–95.

18. Gabaccia, *We Are What We Eat: Ethnic Food and the Making of Americans* (Cambridge, Mass.: Harvard University Press, 1998).

19. Ibid., 217.

20. Julie Salamon, "Chefs Battle Like Samurai in a Cult Hit: Food Network Dishes Up Frog-Fish Crème Brûlée," *New York Times,* June 19, 2000, B1: 6.

21. Jeff Yang, Dina Gan, Terry Hong, et al., *Eastern Standard Time* (Boston: Houghton Mifflin, 1997), 156.

22. Tom Stockley, "Lighter, Tamer Varieties Pair Best with Bold Asian Flavors," *Seattle Times,* October 9, 1996, F2.

23. Zakaria, "The Spice of Your Life: What to drink with Eastern food," *http://www.dsuper.net/-tonbo/asiandrink.html.*

24. Yang, Gan, Hong, et al., *Eastern Standard Time,* 182–187, is an excellent source on East Asian martial arts in the United States.

25. Chris Ballard, "To Class, Kicking and Screaming," *New York Times,* May 5, 2000, B47.

26. Mitchell Tischler, "Karate Kicking Through Summer," *The Almanac* (Potomac, Maryland), August 2–8, 2000, 17.

27. Stephen J. Gould, "The Import of Asian Sexual Psychotechnologies into the United States: The 'New Woman' and 'New Man' Go 'Tantric,'" *Journal of American Culture,* 14 (1991), 19–23.

28. Mark Mitchell, "Tradition at Risk," *Far East Economic Review,* July 20, 2000, 37.

29. "Shaq Is the Talk of the Town," *New York Times,* April 23, 2000, 8: 2.

30. See, for example, my *East Asian Art and American Culture* (New York: Columbia University Press, 1992).

31. Guy Trebay, "Tokyo Street Fashion in New York Bows to No Horizon," *New York Times,* May 23, 2000, A22.

32. Tam, *China Chic* (New York: Regan/HarperCollins, 2000). Tam has also promoted Chinese string-facials for avoiding wrinkles and Chinese spoon massage for ridding the body of toxins. *New York Times,* December 31, 2000, IX: 1, 6.

33. Jane Gross, "The New Game at Elementary School: Picking Your Child's Teacher," *New York Times,* July 16, 2000, 23.

34. George F. Will, "What the Bobos Are Buying," *Washington Post,* April 9, 2000, B7.

35. Matt Richel, "Finding the Alignment For E-Commerce Impact," *New York Times,* April 17, 2000, C4.

36. John F. Mahoney, *The Tao of the Jump Shot: An Eastern Approach to Life and Basketball* (Ulysses Press/Seastone, 1999), with an introduction by NBA Hall of Famer Bill Walton.

37. Cohen, *East Asian Art and American Culture.*

38. Joshua C. Taylor, *The Fine Arts in America* (Chicago: University of Chicago Press, 1979), 154.

39. Zeng Youhe, "Chinese Painting Overseas," in Mayching Kao, ed., *Twentieth Century Chinese Painting* (Hong Kong: Oxford University Press, 1988), 227.

40. Ray Kass, *Morris Graves: Vision of the Inner Eye* (New York: George Braziller, 1983), provides excellent biographical information on Graves.

41. Ibid., 75.

42. As did Janice Prichard Cohen, another Northwest artist.

43. *Washington Post,* May 28, 2000, G3.

44. Jo Ann Lewis, "In New York, Nam June Paik's Video Mojo," *Washington Post,* February 27, 2000, G8.

45. Ann Wilson Lloyd, "Binding Together Cultures with Cords of Wit," *New York Times,* June 18, 2000, AR35.

46. Dore Ashton, *Noguchi East and West* (Berkeley: University of California Press, 1992), is a superb biography and is the basis for my discussion of Noguchi's life.

47. Lancaster, *The Japanese Influence in America* (New York: Walton H. Rawls, 1963).

48. Allan Kozinn, "John Cage, 79, a Minimalist Enchanted with Sound, Dies," *New York Times,* April 13, 1992, A1; John Rockwell, "Cage Merely An Inventor? Not a Chance," *New York Times,* August 23, 1992, II: 21; Edward Rothstein, "Cage Played His Anarchy by the Rules," *New York Times,* September 20, 1992, II: 21.

49. Philip Kennicot, "Bright Sheng's New Quartet Speaks For Itself," *Washington Post,* April 21, 2000, C1, 5.

50. Allan Kozinn, "Chinese-Born Composer Wins $225,000 Ives Prize," *New York Times,* December 21, 2000, B11.

51. A. J. Hewat, "He's Got Rhythm, They've Got Moves: It's a Fit," *New York Times,* June 25, 2000, AR23; Anna Kisselgoff,

"Propelled into Motion by Japanese Drums," *New York Times,* June 29, 2000, B5.

52. Ellen Tomson, "In St. Paul, the Year of 'The Dragon,'" *Washington Post,* July 22, 2000, C4.

53. Seth Mydans, "Khmer Dance in a Lesson for Khmer Rouge," *New York Times,* May 2, 2000, B1.

54. Unless otherwise noted, Richard Hughes Seager, *Buddhism in America* (New York: Columbia University Press, 1999), and Charles B. Prebish and Kenneth K. Tanaka (eds.), *The Faces of Buddhism in America* (Berkeley: University of California Press, 1998), are my sources on American Buddhism.

55. David Shields, "The Good Father," *New York Times Magazine,* April 23, 2000, 60.

56. Gustav Niebuhr, "Spreading Zen on the Prison Grapevine," *New York Times,* May 30, 2001, C17.

57. Adrienne Cook, "Festival at the Temple," *Washington Post,* June 28, 2000, F1, 9.

58. Gustav Niebuhr, "Political Notoriety Puts Light on Buddhist Trend: Asian Faith Enters American Mainstream," *New York Times,* April 29, 2000, A7.

59. Ellen H. Tamura, *Americanization, Acculturation, and Ethnic Identity: The Nisei Generation in Hawaii* (Urbana: University of Illinois Press, 1994); Wayne Patterson, *The Korean Frontier in America: Immigration to Hawaii, 1896–1910* (Honolulu: University of Hawaii Press, 1988).

60. Bill Ong Hing, *Making and Remaking Asian America Through Immigration Policy, 1850–1990* (Stanford: Stanford University Press, 1993), is exceptionally useful.

61. I am indebted to Akira Iriye, whose grandchildren are Irish and Japanese American, for this observation.

62. Stuart Elliott, "Ads Speak to Asian-Americans," *New York Times*, March 6, 2000, C1, 12.

63. David Nakamura, "The Asian Advantage: Suddenly, It's Great To Be Me," *Washington Post*, February 27, 2000, B5.

64. Peter Pae, "Change by the Books: Libraries Respond to Immigrants in an Array of Languages," *Washington Post*, April 26, 2000, B1.

65. Gustav Niebuhr, "A Leader's New Focus: Reconciling Differences," *New York Times*, July 2, 2000, 13.

66. Niebuhr, "Vietnamese Immigrants Swell Catholic Clergy: Growing Influence on a Changing Church," ibid., A11.

67. Lucie Cheng, "Chinese Americans in the Formation of the Pacific Regional Economy," in Evelyn Hu-DeHart (ed.), *Across the Pacific: Asian Americans and Globalization* (Philadelphia: Temple University Press, 1999), 69; see also Hu-Dehart, Introduction, 18–19.

68. James Huntley Grayson, *Korea: A Religious History* (Oxford: Clarendon Press, 1989), 247–250; Marc Fisher and Jeff Leen, "Stymied in U.S., Moon's Church Sounds a Retreat," *Washington Post*, November 24, 1997, A1.

69. Glazer and Moynihan, *Ethnicity: Theory and Experience* (Cambridge, Mass.: Harvard University Press, 1975).

70. Nancy Bernkopf Tucker, *Taiwan, Hong Kong and the United States, 1945–1992: Uncertain Friendships* (New York: Twayne, 1994), 183.

71. Ellen Lee, "A Multicultural Coup at U-Md," *Washington Post*, August 30, 2000, B1, 4.

72. Yossi Shain, "Ethnic Diasporas and U.S. Foreign Policy," *Political Science Quarterly*, 109 (Winter 1994–95), 811–841.

73. Myron Weiner, "Asian Immigrants and U.S. Foreign Policy," in Robert W. Tucker et al., *Immigration and U.S. Foreign Policy* (Boulder: Westview, 1990), 192–213.

74. Xiao-huang Yin and Zhiyong Lan, "Chinese Americans: A Rising Factor in U.S.-China Relations," *Journal of American-East Asian Relations,* 6 (Spring 1997), 35–57.

75. Flier for May 24, 2000, meeting at U.S. Department of State.

76. James Glanz, "Asian-American Scholars Call for Boycott of Labs," *New York Times,* May 31, 2000, A23.

77. Michael A. Fletcher, "Asian Americans Using Politics as a Megaphone: Growing Population Confronts Bias," *Washington Post,* October 2, 2000, 3.

78. Wang, "Roots and Changing Identity of the Chinese in the United States," *Daedalus,* 120 (1991), 181–206.

79. Linda W. Gordon, "Asian Immigration Since World War II," in Tucker et al., *Immigration and U.S. Foreign Policy,* 186.

80. Thomas E. Ricks, "For Pentagon, Asia Moving to Forefront," *Washington Post,* May 26, 2000, 1, 28.

81. The Pulitzer Prize–winning historian Walter A. McDougall, writing perhaps too sanguinely about the effects of the Vietnam War on the United States, suggested that "the deepest long-term effect on America may stem from the rich and undeserved contributions made to American life by the Vietnamese refugees who quietly went to work restoring blighted neighborhoods, building businesses and sending their children to college." *New York Times,* April 26, 2000, A27.

82. Asian American novelists such as Maxine Hong Kingston, Amy Tan, Jessica Hagedorn, Gish Jen, Lois-Ann Yamanaka, and Rahna Reiko Rizzuto have had an enormous impact on contemporary American writing as evidenced by the critical literature they have stimulated.

INDEX